In "Wise Up! Unlock Experience and Make Age an Advantage," Christian Jerusalem offers practical strategies for leveraging the wisdom of experienced workers to drive innovation and growth. His step-by-step approach is easy to follow and demonstrates how harnessing demographic change is possible for every company. This book is an illuminating read for anyone interested in future-proofing their company.

Bettina Dietsche, Chief People and Culture Officer for the Allianz Group

"Wise Up!" addresses one of the most crucial yet often overlooked aspects of talent management today. Senior talents bring a wealth of experience and knowledge and may have different needs regarding their working environment. The book delves into the organization's ability to provide optimal working conditions for employees at the later stage of their career. This will increasingly become a key success factor for many companies and should therefore be a central part of any people strategy.

"Wise Up!" offers numerous suggestions on unlocking the potential of an aging workforce in a comprehensive manner. It explores areas such as job flexibility, development opportunities, knowledge preservation, role adaptation, and cross-generational coaching, providing deep insights into this vital aspect of Wise talent management. The insights provided in this book are profound, making it a must-read for any leader who aims to get ready for the "Silver Tsunami."

Dr. Sven Sommerlatte, CHRO C.H. Boehringer Sohn AG & Co. KG

The unprecedented demographic age shift signals massive change for every organization in the years ahead. From transformational approaches to talent management to the design and manufacture of innovative, age-forward products and services, leaders focused on the future would be well advised to read and respond to Jerusalem's call to action.

Paul Irving, Senior Advisor, Milken Institute; Distinguished Scholar-in-Residence, University of Southern California Leonard Davis School of Gerontology

"Wise Up!" is a game-changing guide for leaders determined to harness the full power of age and experience within their organizations. By breaking down barriers and fostering true collaboration, this book shows how uniting the wisdom of seasoned professionals with the fresh perspectives of new talent can ignite real transformation and drive innovation. Treating intergenerational diversity as a vital asset, "Wise Up!" offers practical strategies to build a culture where every voice is valued and sustainable change becomes possible. If you're ready to lead lasting progress and unlock your team's collective potential, "Wise Up!" is the essential starting point.

Martin Krengel, CEO of the WEPA Group

Wise Up!

Unlock Experience and Make Age an Advantage

Christian Jerusalem

Wise Up!

I am deeply grateful to my wife, Marie, and co-founder of WiseForce Advisors for having the vision, foresight, and belief throughout this journey. Her expertise and unwavering commitment have been instrumental in shaping the ideas in this book.

Thank you for your trust, collaboration, and for making every challenge an opportunity to grow together. Your unwavering belief in me made every page possible.

Table of Contents

Part One: The Silver Tsunami

Part Three: The Age of Wisdom

Part Four: The Platinum Age

Part One:

The Silver
Tsunami

Chapter 1

Gray Is the New Gold: The Disruptive Challenges of an Unprecedented Demographic Shift

People often ask how I came to specialize in helping organizations tap into the potential of an aging workforce. As a leadership consultant, I've always been fascinated by the idea of experience as an asset. It has never made sense to me why our western society doesn't value the wisdom that comes with age. Over the years, I've observed up-close how this pattern plays out in a wide variety of employment settings. Corporations, nonprofits, and government institutions in countries around the world place all their attention on the youngest employees while they do everything possible to push older workers into early retirement. I believe this is shortsighted decision-making because when experienced people leave a place of work, they take vital skills, knowledge, and insights along with them.

Some years ago, the leaders of a private equity firm invited me to pitch my consulting services for a high-profile management audit after a takeover deal had closed. My team and I presented our proposal to help with this transition, and at the end of the meeting, we posed a question to the executives in the room: Why had they overlooked several core business areas and not nominated anyone from those functions to be considered for the newly combined leadership team? To my way of thinking, these experienced employees would only strengthen the leadership team. The answer came abruptly and left me feeling puzzled: "Those individuals are too old and not part of the future here."

For the last 10 years, I've been on a personal and professional journey to understand what changes as we age, what's the good and bad of being "old," and how different generations can work together in meaningful ways to create business value. To appreciate the importance of this topic, one needs to have a clear picture of the forces that are shaping global population trends and workforce demographics. Let's dive in:

Aging Facts

Let's start by looking at how the world population is expected to grow:

The UN expects the world population to reach 8.5 billion in 2030 and to increase further to 9.7 billion in 2050, reaching some 10.4 billion by 2100.[1]

The predictions differ according to assumptions around fertility, mortality, and economic prosperity. In the most extreme scenario, according to data from the Lancet study, the world population could decline by almost 2 billion people to just 6 billion by the end of the century.[2]

This scenario assumes meeting the sustainable development goals' targets for education and contraceptive needs.

By contrast, however, researchers also expect to see regional differences. For example, in the European Union, population is projected to increase from 446.7 million in 2022 and peak at 453.3 million in 2026 (an increase of +1.5 percent), then gradually decrease to 447.9 million in 2050 and to 419.5 million in 2100.[3] Despite its globally significant growth—the world population is also aging. To understand this better, let's examine how the group of people aged 50 and over is projected to expand nearly 70 percent by 2050, rising from 1.9 billion in 2020 to 3.2 billion in 2050. The growth will be strongest in the next decade,

1   https://databank.worldbank.org/source/population-estimates-and-projections
2   https://www.thelancet.com/article/S0140-6736(20)30677-2/fulltext
3   Population projections in the EU—Statistics Explained

reaching 2.3 billion people aged 50+ by 2030. Accordingly, this generation's share of the total population is projected to increase to an unprecedented level—from 24 percent in 2020 to 33 percent by 2050 (see figure below).[4]

To put these numbers into perspective, it took more than twice as long—from 1950 to 2020—for the same kind of shift to take place previously. In 1950, people in the 50+ age bracket comprised just 16 percent of the total population, and by 2020, they accounted for 24 percent.

Global population distribution by age cohort, in 2020 und 2050

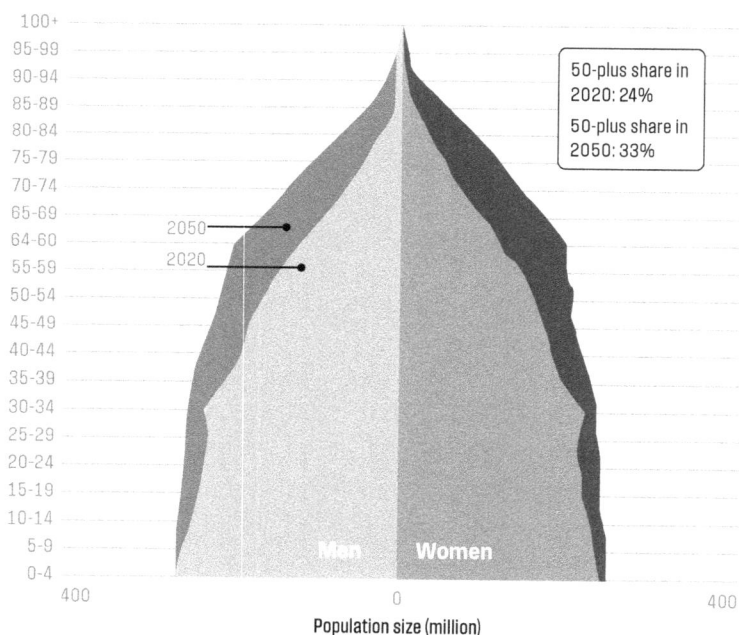

Source: The number of people age 50 and older will grow 69% by 2050

4   https://www.aarp.org/content/dam/aarp/research/surveys_statistics/econ/2022/global-longevity-economy-report.doi.10.26419-2Fint.00052.001.pdf

The demographic change that's in motion now will shape organizations and society for years to come. This shift is as big as climate change, and it's unprecedented in how it's affecting the entire globe. The rapid aging of our worldwide population will have a long-term impact on every individual, as well as the global workforce and economy.

More Demographic Trends

Let's take a closer look at the factors that are driving this remarkable transformation:

Increasing life expectancy: One reason we have an aging global population is that people are living much longer. Between 2000 and 2019, global life expectancy increased by six years, from 67 to 73, and it is projected to reach 77 years by 2050.[5] As the population ages, many countries soon will reach a point at which more people are leaving the workforce than are entering it.

For example, if your company would be in the United Kingdom, that tipping point may be as soon as 2029. In Brazil, the forecast is for 2035; for India, it's 2048; and in the United States more people will be exiting the workforce by 2053.[6]

Advances in healthcare and improved living conditions have led to a substantial increase in life expectancy worldwide. As a result, people are not only living longer but also remaining active and capable of working well into their later years.

According to a Federal Reserve survey, 45 percent of employed older adults consider themselves to be retired while still working.[7] This figure suggests that a significant portion of older workers is engaging in what economists call "bridge jobs"—employment taken after retir-

5   https://databank.worldbank.org/source/population-estimates-and-projections
6   https://www.bbc.com/worklife/article/20240404-global-retirement-increase-65-to-75
7   https://www.pewresearch.org/social-trends/2023/12/14/the-growth-of-the-older-workforce/

ing from a primary career but before fully exiting the workforce. The survey found that these retired older workers are blending work and retirement, rather than making a clean break from employment. The ability to work part-time in less-demanding roles appears to be an important factor enabling continued workforce participation past traditional retirement age. For many older adults, it is a financial necessity to continue working so they can afford the cost of living longer.

What is a "bridge job"?

Employment taken after retiring from a primary career, before an individual fully exits the workforce.

Declining fertility rates: The second driver behind the aging population trend is that women are having fewer children, leaving older adults to account for a higher percentage of the population. As countries develop economically and socially, fertile women of childbearing years tend to have fewer children for several reasons:

- increased access to education and employment opportunities for women
- wider availability of contraception and family planning services
- changing social norms around family size
- higher costs associated with raising children in developed economies

Accordingly, the global fertility rate, measured as births per 1,000 women, declined from 2.7 in 2000 to 2.4 in 2019 and is projected to drop to 2.2 by 2050. In upper-middle-income economies, the fertility rate is 1.8, well below the replacement rate of 2.1 children per woman that is necessary to maintain a stable population, and it is approaching the low rate of 1.7 seen in high-income economies.[8]

---

8   https://databank.worldbank.org/source/population-estimates-and-projections

While global fertility rates are declining overall, some regions are experiencing particularly rapid decreases:
- East Asia: South Korea and Japan are seeing extremely low birth rates.
- Southern Europe: Italy and Spain have struggled with low fertility for decades.
- Eastern Europe: Many countries in this region face a combination of low birth rates and emigration.

When we hear organizations complaining today about the difficulties of finding additional workers, then this is just the beginning, as the effect of global fertility decline is just about to start.

Impact on the Workforce

If the world is faced with declining fertility and with a growing, yet aging population due to longevity, what does this mean for the future of work? This demographic shift is reshaping the labor market, challenging traditional notions of retirement, and forcing businesses to adapt their strategies to accommodate an increasingly multigenerational workforce. Whichever set of statistics you consider, it's clear that fewer young workers will be entering the job market to replace those who are retiring. This reality creates a likely labor shortage that will increase the importance of retaining older workers.

The combined effect of the global decline of the working-age population will be the strongest in the next 25 years. For that reason alone, organizations should be on alert! Look at the chart below for more details:

Working-Age Population

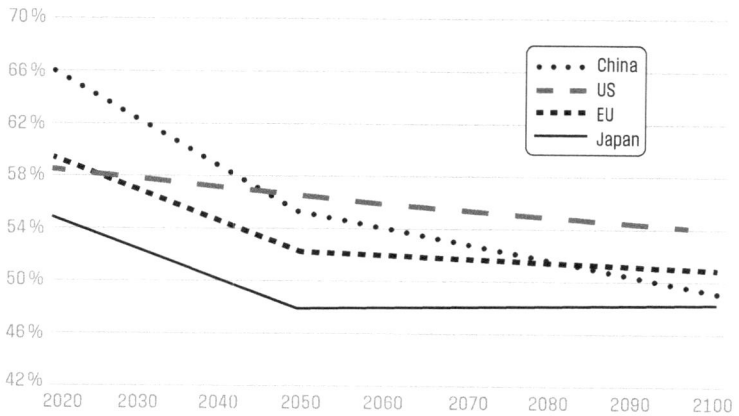

Two notable effects are evident in the workforce:

1. **Extended careers:** The concept of retirement at 65 is becoming outdated. Many individuals are choosing to work longer, either for personal fulfillment or out of financial necessity. This shift means that careers can span multiple decades and potentially multiple fields.

2. **Skills gaps:** As technology advances rapidly, companies have a growing need for workers with up-to-date skills. Older workers may find it challenging to learn new systems, while younger workers may lack the experience and soft skills valued by employers. This situation creates both challenges and opportunities for workforce development. We will explore these developments in more detail in Chapter 10.

Adapting to an Aging Workforce

Many organizations are beginning to implement stopgap efforts to manage the reality of an aging workforce. However, without an overall strategy to guide the way, these initiatives inevitably fall short of solving the root problem.

I believe it's crucial for businesses, policymakers, and individuals to embrace the shift in age distribution and implement supportive policies at a strategic level, so they can harness the full potential of a multigenerational workforce. We know that the working-age population is likely to shrink for a long time to come and, inevitably, this trend will fuel a war for talent. To win that war, companies will need to tap into the valuable experience, stability, and mentorship capabilities that older workers bring to the workplace. And achieving that vision requires leadership commitment, education about the benefits of age diversity, and a long-term approach that considers both the developing trends and the contributions of experienced workers.

Organizations that take the time now to plan strategically around these demographic trends will be in a much better position to achieve their growth, innovation, and productivity objectives. In doing so, they will create a more resilient, innovative, and inclusive labor market that leverages the strengths of workers across all age groups.

Perception vs. Reality of Aging

Jonathan, the energetic, fortysomething CEO of a large machinery company, walked into the office on Monday feeling concerned. Over the weekend, he had reflected on the lack of progress his company was making on its transformation program. The goal of the initiative was to become less hierarchical, both in the way the company was structured and the way its culture was lived. But Jonathan worried that the company's workforce was not embracing the new agile working style and only haphazardly embracing the new matrix organization.

The company had always been proud of its highly skilled workers and their long tenures. Work quality and customer satisfaction remained above industry standards. But as he looked more closely at the organization, Jonathan saw a growing generational divide between younger employees, who welcomed the change, and older ones, who remained apprehensive. In the training program data, Jonathan noted the participation rate of the 50+ age bracket had been significantly lower than that of other age groups. He started to wonder if an improved leadership approach, focused on the needs of an aging workforce, would help.

The aging phenomenon and its implications can be difficult to perceive at first, but the research tells us that, by 2030, approximately 150 million jobs will shift to workers over age 55, constituting a quarter of the workforce.[9]

Some of the common telltales include:

- You notice declining physical and cognitive abilities among your older workers, potentially impacting productivity and increasing the risk of workplace accidents.
- You may experience higher rates of absenteeism due to health issues.
- The company faces a growing skills gap, which develops when older workers retire, without transferring knowledge and skills to younger colleagues.
- You see older employees struggling to learn new technologies without additional support and training.
- Employees report poor team dynamics caused by generational differences.

9   https://ohsonline.com/Articles/2024/07/05/Adapting-Business-Practices-for-an-Aging-Workforce.aspx 5

At the same time, some organizations are becoming aware of the opportunities inherent in an aging workforce, including:[10]

- **Experience and wisdom:** Older workers bring valuable skills, knowledge, and experience to the workplace, which can benefit the organization.
- **Mentorship:** Experienced workers can mentor and train younger employees, facilitating knowledge transfer.
- **Loyalty:** Older workers tend to be more loyal and committed to their employers, potentially reducing turnover rates.
- **Improved safety measures:** Accommodating older workers can lead to the implementation of better safety protocols that benefit all employees.[11]

As companies begin to perceive the reality of their aging employee bases, they may decide to experiment with some of the following changes; this is often a set of disconnected actions, more tactical than strategic in nature:

1. **Flexible work arrangements:** Many employers are offering flexible working conditions, including hours, location, and job-protected time off, which are highly valued by older workers.
2. **Ergonomic workplace design:** Organizations are investing in ergonomic workplaces to reduce employee injuries and minimize absenteeism.
3. **Training and development:** Companies are adjusting their training approaches to ensure information is accessible to all age groups and providing opportunities for older workers to update their skills.
4. **Succession planning:** Organizations are implementing succession planning strategies to minimize knowledge loss due to retirement and to encourage mentorship.

---

10 https://www.econstor.eu/bitstream/10419/302079/1/16-ENTRENOVA-2023.pdf
11 https://www.work-fit.com/blog/aging-workforce-challenges-opportunities

5. **Health and wellness programs:** Some employers are introducing functional capacity wellness programs to ensure workers are physically fit for their roles and can perform tasks safely.

6. **Age-diverse recruitment:** Organizations are recognizing the need to attract and retain both younger and older employees to maintain a balanced workforce.

7. **Phased retirement:** Some companies are offering more refined phased retirement options to extend older workers' participation in the workforce and facilitate better retirement adjustment.

How well prepared is your organization for the aging phenomenon? Here are a few questions to start the conversation which aim at a more comprehensive solution that is rooted in your business strategy to achieve your objectives:

– How would you describe the age narrative in your organization?
– What signs of age bias have you noticed in the company culture and business practices?
– What processes and policies are in place already to support the shift in age distribution in the organization to better achieve your corporate objectives?
– Which factors are holding you back and how would you rate those drag factors accordingly?
– Do you have a strategy in place to leverage the potential of your senior workforce to support the corporate strategy?

How We View and Experience Age in the Workplace

Current research on the perception versus reality of aging in organizations reveals several important insights. For starters, we can see that congruence between leaders' and older employees' perceptions of age-friendly organizational practices positively impacts employees' sense of fulfillment. When both leaders and older workers perceive high levels of age-friendliness, older people trust their leaders more, which enhances attitudes, behavior, and wellbeing.[12]

Conversely, when leaders overestimate the age-friendliness of their organizational practices compared to how their older employees perceive the practices, it can lead to negative outcomes, such as decreased fulfillment and trust among older employees.

Older workers often internalize societal age norms and stereotypes, which influence their decisions about extending their working lives or retiring. These norms can lead to a sense of "intergenerational disentitlement," in which older workers feel they should leave opportunities to younger colleagues.[13] Moreover, the internalization of negative age stereotypes can affect older workers' motivation for training and development, reinforcing managerial biases that exclude them from such opportunities.[14]

A growing body of research now shows that perceived age discrimination increases with age and is associated with lower job satisfaction, poorer self-rated health, and higher depressive symptoms among older workers. This discrimination can also influence retirement decisions, as older employees may choose to leave organizations in which they feel discriminated against. Adding to the complexity, implicit measures reveal stable negative biases against older workers that may not be captured by explicit measurements of ageism in the workplace.[15]

The lived experience of aging is changing, with many older adults maintaining productivity and health well into later life. However, societal perceptions have not kept pace with these changes and, too often, age continues to be viewed through a lens of decline. There is a growing movement toward "positive" or "successful aging," which

12 https://academic.oup.com/workar/article/10/2/123/7111320
13 https://www.frontiersin.org/journals/sociology/articles/10.3389/fsoc.2021.686645/full
14 https://www.allgpsy2.uni-jena.de/data/rothdata/PCR19.pdf
15 https://www.allgpsy2.uni-jena.de/data/rothdata/PCR19.pdf

encourages maintaining productivity, health, and autonomy in later life. This movement aims to counteract negative stereotypes associated with aging.

Even so, an AARP survey from 2022 found that approximately 80 percent of American workers between ages 40 and 65 reported either witnessing or personally experiencing age discrimination at work.[16] And in Germany, 11 percent of older workers reported ageism in 2023, highlighting systemic issues in the job market that undervalue individuals as they age.[17]

Overall, this research underscores the importance of addressing both the perceptions and realities of aging within organizations to foster a more inclusive and supportive work environment for older employees.

What is ageism?

The term "ageism" was originally coined by Robert Neil Butler in 1969. Ageism refers to the bias, discrimination, or harassment against individuals and groups based on their age.

The Taboo of Aging

In the bustling offices of the Water Corporation, a silent divide grew deeper with each passing day. Sarah, a brilliant 58-year-old marketing executive, found herself increasingly isolated from team meetings and decision-making processes. Younger colleagues whispered about her "outdated" ideas, unaware of the wealth of experience she brought to the table.

16 https://www.bbc.com/worklife/article/20240320-gen-x-workplace-ageism
17 https://totalent.eu/discrimination-still-plagues-the-german-labour-market/

Meanwhile, in the IT department, a 25-year-old prodigy named Alex struggled to have his innovative solutions taken seriously. "You're too young to understand the complexities," his manager would say, dismissing his ideas without a second thought.

As the company prepared for its annual strategy meeting, both Sarah and Alex were conspicuously absent from the invite list. The boardroom buzzed with talk of "fresh perspectives" and "digital natives," while decades of accumulated wisdom sat untapped just a few cubicles away.

In the break room, frequent conversations about retirement and "making way for the next generation" created an atmosphere of unease among older employees. Sarah and her peers began to feel like relics, their contributions overshadowed by stereotypes of inflexibility and technological ineptitude.

The impact of this unspoken ageism rippled through the organization. Productivity suffered as valuable insights were lost, and a sense of disengagement spread among workers of all ages. The once-collaborative spirit of Water Corporation gave way to age-based cliques that hindered innovation and teamwork.

As the fiscal year came to a close, Water Corporation's leadership remained oblivious to the true cost of their age-biased culture. They failed to see that, by marginalizing both their oldest and youngest talent, they were writing a story of missed opportunities and untapped potential.

The taboo of aging at the Water Corporation wasn't just about discrimination; it was a silent thief, robbing the company of its most valuable asset—the diverse perspectives and experiences of its multigenerational workforce.

Despite increasing awareness of demographic trends and the likely impact on organizations, aging continues to be thought of as a negative—something to be avoided at all costs. If you want to know what this looks like in day-to-day work life, start with your organization's hiring practices, the most common source of age discrimination in business.

In a survey of New Zealand workers, 85 percent of respondents believed it will become increasingly difficult to secure employment as they age.[18] This manifests in several ways:

- Younger hiring managers may favor candidates closer to their own age, perceiving them as more likely to stay with the company longer.
- Job descriptions and recruitment materials may use language that subtly discourages older applicants ("High-energy individual needed for a fast-paced environment").
- Some older workers even report feeling compelled to alter their appearances, such as dyeing their hair, to appear younger during job interviews.

Negative stereotypes about older workers contribute to the bias. For example, older employees may be perceived as less competent or adaptable, despite their wealth of experience. And there's a misconception that older workers are less tech-savvy and more resistant to change,[19] despite the fact that they are not universally this way.[20] And older women face a "double whammy" of both sexism and ageism, with visible signs of aging affecting perceptions of their competence and attractiveness.

For all these reasons, as employees age, they may face considerable challenges in career progression and job security. Older workers might be passed over for promotions or professional development opportunities, especially in industries that are perceived as "youth-oriented" like events and marketing. The "thinning out" of older employees in higher positions suggests a systemic issue with retaining experienced workers: A 2023 study by McKinsey & Company found that nearly a third of newly appointed S&P 500 CEOs in 2022 were younger than 50, which is more than twice the rate observed in 2018.[21] This trend

---

18 https://capsulenz.com/thrive/ageism-in-the-workplace/
19 https://seniorsatwork.nz/blog/the-age-taboo-in-workplaces-means-we-miss-out-on-talent/
20 https://www.hrfuture.net/talent-management/technology/older-workers-and-tech-2021-study/
21 https://www.bbc.com/worklife/article/20230727-are-gen-z-ready-for-leadership

indicates a significant increase in younger individuals taking on top leadership positions in major corporations.

The taboo around aging shapes workplace culture and creates an uncomfortable work environment for older employees. Ageist jokes or comments may be more tolerated than other forms of discrimination. Older workers might feel pressure to hide their ages or downplay their experience to fit in. And workplace policies and practices may unintentionally favor younger employees, such as with inflexible work arrangements that don't accommodate the needs of older workers.

Perhaps the most insidious aspect of the aging taboo is the silence surrounding it. Ashton Applewhite, a famous voice in the US who has raised awareness of this issue, describes ageism as "the last socially acceptable prejudice,"[22] indicating a lack of awareness and action compared to other forms of discrimination. Many older workers struggle to prove age discrimination, so it becomes difficult to address the issue openly. And while organizations say they have diversity and inclusivity initiatives, age frequently gets overlooked in these efforts.

The taboo of aging has legal implications, too. Younger workers tend to be perceived as more desirable;[23] yet any organization that tries to shape its workforce according to age-related criteria becomes subject to legal scrutiny.

In 2024, the US Bureau of Labor Statistics projected that there will be an increase in workers aged 55 and older, including a rise in those older than 65, as a percentage of the overall workforce. Age-related litigation in the workplace is also spiking, especially allegations of age-related harassment and discrimination.[24]

By recognizing and addressing the taboo of aging in the workplace, companies in any country can begin to create more inclusive environments that value the contributions of workers across all age groups.

22 https://www.ted.com/talks/ashton_applewhite_let_s_end_ageism
23 https://www.emerald.com/insight/content/doi/10.1108/ijm-10-2018-0358/full/html
24 https://advocacy.calchamber.com/2024/07/17/age-related-litigation-challenges-in-to-days-workplace/

Given the increasingly challenging business environments in the world, organizations will benefit from leveraging the assets of the entire workforce. In light of better business outcomes, it simply makes sense to tap into the potential of your experienced workforce. Why not apply this healthy business mindset and accelerate your performance?

An Emerging Generational Divide

For the first time in history, many workplaces span six generations, from the octogenarians of the Silent Generation (80 years and older)—who are still working in key global leadership roles—to the teenagers of the emerging Generation Alpha, who are eagerly pursuing their first summer jobs and high school internships. In between, we have the Baby Boomers, Generation X, Generation Y (often called the Millennials), and Generation Z, representing practically the entire workforce.[25]

This is an unprecedented age span, and it's a real challenge for organizations to manage because each generation is distinctly different in its character and expectations. It is critically important for organiza-

		BOOMER	GEN X	MILLENNIAL	GEN Z
✺	Chronology	1946-1964	1965-1981	1982-1996	1997-2012
🔒	Key Moments	Marshall Plan, Civil Rights, Sexual Revolution	Berlin Wall, Watergate, Energy Crisis, Downsizing	Child Focused, Divorce Norm	Digital Norm, 9/11, GFC, UN Climate Report
⚙	Work is	Adventure, then Retire	A Job, a Contract	Means to End, Values	Entrepreneur Purpose
💎	Values	Status + Achievement	Freedom + Responsibility	Experiences	Improve the World

Source: The Empathy Advantage, Heather McGowan, Chris Shipley, 2024

---

25   https://hbr.org/2024/04/leading-the-6-generation-workforce?registration=success

tional leaders to understand the defining moments for each age group, what "work" means for each of them, and what values motivate their behavior and decision-making.

Let's consider each generation in more detail:[26]

Boomers (b. 1946–1964): In the United States currently, Baby Boomers make up about 15 percent of the labor force. Their participation has been declining as more of this generation reaches retirement age.

Generation X (b. 1965–1981): Gen X comprises approximately 31 percent to 36 percent of the workforce. This group represents a significant portion of the labor force, often occupying middle and senior management positions.

Generation Y (b. 1982–1996): Millennials currently make up the largest share of the workforce, accounting for about 36 percent to 40 percent of all workers. Gen Y has overtaken other generations in workforce participation.

Generation Z (b. 1997–2012): Gen Z's presence in the workforce is growing rapidly. Young workers now make up about 18 percent of the labor force, having recently surpassed Baby Boomers in workforce participation.

Who is 50+?

Technically, the "50+" category represents a mix of the Boomers and Gen X employees. In many organizations, about 30 percent of the workforce is 50 years and older. In G7 countries, workers aged 55 and older are projected to exceed 25 percent of the workforce by 2031, an increase of nearly 10 percentage points from 2011. Globally, it's estimated that approximately 150 million jobs will shift to workers 55 and older by the end of this decade.

---

26 https://www.dol.gov/sites/dolgov/files/ETA/opder/DASP/Trendlines/posts/2024_08/Trendlines_August_2024.html

The generational divide shows up in a few different ways at work. Here are a few examples you may recognize:[27]

Communication styles: Different generations have distinct preferences for communication methods. A survey by BridgeWorks found that 72 percent of Millennials prefer digital communication channels, while 50 percent of Baby Boomers prefer face-to-face communication. This disparity can lead to misunderstandings and inefficiencies in the workplace.

Work expectations: Each generation has different expectations regarding work-life balance, career development, and job stability. For instance, Gen X tends to value flexibility and autonomy, while Millennials often seek mentorship and purpose in their work.

Technological proficiency: Younger generations like Millennials and Gen Z are typically more adept with the latest technologies, while Baby Boomers and some Gen Xers may require additional training and support.

Attitudes toward authority and collaboration: Baby Boomers often prefer more hierarchical structures, which can clash with Millennials' preference for collaborative approaches.

Looking at the landscape of an aging workforce and a widening generational divide, leaders should consider taking these six steps to prepare:

1. **Bridge communication gaps:** Implement strategies that accommodate diverse communication preferences to ensure effective collaboration across all age groups.[28]

2. **Manage resistance to change:** Older generations may resist changes that younger employees embrace, requiring clear communication about the benefits of change and involving team members in transition processes.

27 https://greco.services/leading-diverse-teams-challenges-of-various-generations/
28 https://humansmart.com.mx/en/blogs/blog-what-are-the-key-challenges-of-managing-a-multigenerational-workforce-57659

3. **Address skills gaps:** As technology evolves, skills gaps can emerge between generations, necessitating ongoing training and development programs.
4. **Foster inclusive culture:** Creating an environment in which every generation feels valued is crucial. A survey by LinkedIn revealed that 89 percent of employees believe a strong team culture significantly reduces workplace conflicts.[29]
5. **Retain talent across generations:** With Millennials frequently changing jobs and Gen Z seeking entrepreneurial opportunities, companies need to balance their workforces across the generations.
6. **Support mental health and wellbeing:** A survey by the American Psychological Association found that Millennials and Gen Z report higher levels of stress compared to older generations, highlighting the need for mental health support in the workplace.[30]

Managing the growing group of 50+ workers effectively presents a strategic opportunity for organizations to reposition around intergenerational inclusion and impact for the long term. At the same time, if executives are unwilling or unprepared to engage this new multigenerational reality, organizational chaos and decline may ensue.

What to Do

Craft a generational strategy to support your organization's objectives. Task leaders with creating the conditions that incentivize older and younger workers alike to be open to learning from and with one another, sharing their wisdom and know-how without fear or insecurity.

Engage in succession planning—it is essential for organizational sustainability. Given the intergenerational challenges, organizations

---

29   https://vorecol.com/blogs/blog-what-are-the-key-challenges-of-managing-generational-diversity-and-how-can-leaders-effectively-address-them-141717
30   https://greco.services/leading-diverse-teams-challenges-of-various-generations/

will benefit from looking into how to become employers-of-choice for every generation (not just the younger ones), anchored by a compelling brand that is both authentic and attentive to each generation's needs and preferences.

Actively manage differences that could be aged-based or generational. Remember, age-based differences refer to where an individual is within their lifespan, while generations are cohorts of people who were born at a similar time and have been shaped by common historical and cultural experiences and/or forces in their formative years. Multigenerational teams often experience interpersonal tensions, such as differences in norms regarding the use of technology, communication styles around giving and receiving feedback, and ideas of what "hard work" and "good leadership" look like. Instead of falling into the trap of stereotyping, judging, and then attempting to "fix" the other generations, these differences can be viewed as cultural attributes. This approach paves the way to acknowledging generational differences without dividing them from one another.

Rally around a shared purpose. The most powerful intergenerational unifier is the organization's purpose—defined as "an aspirational reason for being which inspires and provides a call to action for an organization and its partners and stakeholders, and provides benefit to local and global society," according to the Harvard Business Review.[31] Take the time to articulate the fundamental reason for the company's existence beyond just generating profit, and you'll be amazed by how it shifts the focus to what we have in common, rather than what divides us. While fostering the organizational sense of purpose, leaders can also help employees to activate their own personal sense of purpose while coming together with others to fulfill the organization's vision and mission at the same time.

---

31 https://www.breathehr.com/en-gb/blog/topic/business-leadership/how-can-you-deliver-organisational-purpose

CHAPTER 1 SUMMARY

Demographic changes in the global workforce are bringing about a significant transformation as populations age and people
live longer, healthier lives. It is paramount
for organizations to adapt to the reality of
an aging workforce. We all need to challenge perceptions and change our organizational processes and policies to meet
the needs of older workers and the emerging generational divide. Ignoring or not
sufficiently addressing these trends will
compromise innovation, competitiveness,
and productivity.

Chapter 2
The Silver Dollar: Economic Realities of an Aging Workforce

The Drift Phenomenon

On a November day, Caroline sat at her desk, staring at the computer screen and reflecting on her time with the employer she'd served for more than two decades. "I was hired to be a marketing specialist, and at first, I was eager, full of ambition. Over the years, I became known as the go-to person for campaign strategy. My colleagues often joke that I can predict consumer trends in my sleep," she says.

For a long time, Caroline felt a deep sense of pride in her work. She belonged to this place and always felt that her contributions were valued. But lately, something seemed off. The familiar routine that she once enjoyed was beginning to feel constrictive. At 53, she found herself asking, "Is this all there is for me professionally? I looked around at the younger faces, buzzing with excitement over the latest company strategy and wondered if I even belonged anymore."

As time passed, Caroline grew more sensitive to the changes happening around her. A reorganization here, a new policy there—each one felt like a potential threat to her status, her autonomy, and her relationships at work. A nagging worry kept her up at night: "Do I still matter?"

She started looking for signs that the company still valued her expertise—an opportunity to lead a new project or shift her role to something new. She would even welcome an invitation to learn new skills in a professional training program. But those signs never came. Instead, Caroline felt taken for granted. Her boss acted as though the company had invested enough in her and now it was time for her to deliver. "It was a subtle shift from my performance being valued, to being simply expected," she recalls.

Understandably, Caroline began to withdraw mentally. Her colleagues didn't seem to notice at first, but she felt herself drifting away. "It's not that I don't care anymore—it's just that I'm not sure if anyone else does. And in this state of limbo, I find myself wondering what the next chapter of my career will look like, and whether it will be written here or somewhere else entirely."

Caroline's story is an all too common one, and when professionals like her start to withdraw mentally and emotionally from their employers, we refer to the phenomenon as "drifting." Drifting happens when "nine to five" replaces "going the extra mile." Drifters still do their jobs, but in a reactive mode. They observe the changes around them, and instead of looking for new opportunities, they focus on protecting the status quo. It's an effective coping mechanism to deal with setbacks and lack of inclusion and appreciation. Eroding productivity from drifting employees may be hard to detect, but it builds up over time and can become a systemic issue before you know it.

What is Drifting?

Drifting refers to the experience that older people inside an organization have when they no longer feel committed or attached. This happens when a company no longer gives attention to an individual because of a conscious or unconscious bias against investing in someone "older" and/or who may be expected to leave the company at an undefined time in the future, perhaps through early retirement.

Cost and Productivity Impact of Older Workers

We've all encountered proactive individuals in the workplace. They plan ahead and prioritize tasks effectively. They are always looking for ways to improve processes and prevent issues, and this approach creates an environment for innovation and creativity to thrive. Drifters tend to lose their formerly proactive inclinations and settle into a reactive, defensive mode. This change has a significant impact on productivity and costs organizations a lot of money.

Are older workers more costly than younger ones, simply because of their age? Not necessarily. The perception of older workers as a major cost impediment to business is greatly exaggerated and not supported by current evidence. When people costs go up, it's often due to a preventable decline in productivity. If leaders don't allow the drifting phenomenon to take hold, they can reap the cost-savings benefits of keeping experienced workers in the mix.

Let's take a closer look:

Productivity Considerations

As workers age, their productivity may start to decline due to physical or cognitive changes or inability/unwillingness to use the latest technologies. For example, a study on Japanese workers found that productivity peaked for those in their 40s and declined thereafter. This aging effect may have reduced Japan's annual total factor productivity growth by 0.7–0.9 percentage point between 1990 and 2005.[32]

Moody's Analytics published a study on Aging and Productivity[33] in 2018 that found "no definitive conclusions as to the mechanisms causing aging to weigh on productivity, but a plausible theory is that older workers may resist productivity-improving technologies. Understanding why older workers are reducing productivity growth is essential if ways to mitigate the effects are to be found."

An aging workforce also can lead to higher costs for employers due to increased healthcare expenses, higher wages, absenteeism, caregiv-

32 https://www.imf.org/en/Blogs/Articles/2016/12/09/why-productivity-growth-is-faltering-in-aging-europe-and-japan
33 https://ma.moodys.com/rs/961-KCJ-308/images/2018-09-04-Aging-and-the-Productivity-Puzzle.pdf

ing responsibilities, and age-related workplace accommodations such as modified schedules. At the same time, older workers tend to stay in their jobs longer than younger peers, they show higher levels of work commitment, and are more reliable. Contrary to popular opinion, they often demonstrate the ability to acquire new skills and contribute creative ideas.

The relationship between age and productivity is not straightforward. Encourage Equality, a promoter of age neutrality at work, cites a number of insights:[34] According to a recent EU report, "There is no empirical evidence that older workers are more or less productive than other age groups." While some studies suggest a potential decline in productivity with age, this is often offset by experience and job-specific knowledge.

Moreover, older workers often provide cost-saving benefits that offset any potential higher wages. Workers aged over 55 are five times less likely to change jobs compared to workers aged 20 to 24, reducing recruitment and training costs. Older workers have lower rates of absenteeism, providing a greater return on training investments. And they demonstrate higher levels of work commitment, reliability, and the ability to acquire new skills.

Compensation Trends
Modern compensation practices have reduced age-based wage differences, as evidenced by these statistics: 90 percent of large companies now use performance-based variable compensation rather than tenure-based compensation, up from 78 percent in 2005.

Flexible Work Arrangements
Companies can leverage older workers' expertise cost-effectively through flexible work hours, contract positions, or part-time roles, allowing companies to access their expertise at lower costs. These

---

34 https://encourageequality.au/equality/dreamin

arrangements can be mutually beneficial for both companies and older workers.

In conclusion, while there may be a small element of truth to older workers being more expensive in some cases, this is outweighed by the benefits these workers contribute and changing compensation structures. The traditional and simplified belief that older workers are more costly than younger ones is not correct. However, if the aging workforce is not managed well, insufficient leadership of mature workers will lead to the "drift" phenomenon. And having a lot of drifters in your organization is going to be a burden on your bottom line. By proactively managing an aging workforce, I believe companies can mitigate productivity losses and leverage the valuable experience of older workers.

Ageism

The economic impact of ageism on the overall economy and organization is staggering: According to an AARP (American Association of Retired People) study, age discrimination in American workplaces cost the US economy an estimated $850 billion in gross domestic product (GDP) in 2018.[35] This figure is roughly equivalent to the size of Pennsylvania's entire economy. By 2050, these losses could potentially climb to $3.9 trillion, comparable to the current GDP of Germany.[36]

Ageist practices, such as forced early retirement or limited opportunities for older workers, lead to inefficient use of human resources and skills, and can eventually lead to a decline in GDP. In Australia, for example, it's estimated that, if 5 percent more people aged 55 or older were employed, it would have a positive impact of AUD$48 billion annually on the national economy.

---

35 https://www.elcmd.org/post/cost-of-age-discrimination
36 https://www.aarp.org/politics-society/advocacy/info-2020/age-discrimination-economic-impact.html

Likewise, a Stepstone study[37] showed that the German labor market could retain around 570,000 more workers annually from 2030 to 2035, if those reaching retirement age chose to continue working. This would correspond to a potential increase in German GDP of up to 0.7 percent per year on average, based on 2023 GDP figures. This projection is based on data showing that approximately 39 percent of workers aged 55 and older want to work beyond retirement age.

Ageism & Health

Experiencing ageism may also affect one's overall health. The United States spends billions of dollars per year treating health conditions attributable to ageism. This increased healthcare spend puts a strain on the overall healthcare system and economy. The World Health Organization now estimates that roughly 6 million cases of depression globally may be attributable to ageism.[38]

Ageism also affects social cohesion and intergenerational relations, leading to withdrawal and social isolation. Loneliness among older adults could also weaken community ties. This often correlates with a fading autonomy of older individuals.[39] From all these studies and more, we have overwhelming evidence that ageism affects the overall wellbeing of the population.[40]

What About the Cost to Companies?

Ageist practices impair organizational productivity and innovation in numerous ways:

Productivity: Companies that demonstrate ageist practices miss out on the valuable experience and knowledge that older workers bring

---

37 https://www.thestepstonegroup.com/english/newsroom/press-releases/delaying-retire-ment-boost-for-the-economy-28-billion-euros-potential-per-year-for-germany/

38 https://www.helpguide.org/aging/healthy-aging/ageism-and-age-discrimination

39 https://joint-research-centre.ec.europa.eu/jrc-news-and-updates/addressing-age-ism-key-priority-society-longevity-2024-07-11_en

40 https://www.google.com/url?q=https://www.who.int/health-topics/ageism&sa=D&source=docs&ust=1741693167572602&usg=AOvVaw14i2RbtHEEqIQDjvHSs_kf

to the table. This results in a substantial loss of productivity and innovation potential.[41] Diverse perspectives and experiences drive innovation, and an age-diverse workforce is better equipped to understand and serve a diverse customer base, potentially leading to increased market share and customer satisfaction.

Problem-solving: The combination of skills and knowledge from different generations also enhances an organization's problem-solving capabilities. Older employees often bring deep industry insights, while younger employees may contribute fresh ideas and technological proficiency. Together, they can complement each other's skill sets, boosting the company's innovative potential.

Industry knowledge: By sidelining or dismissing older workers, companies lose access to a wealth of industry knowledge, technical skills, and professional networks that these employees have accumulated over their careers. According to an International Data Corp. (IDC) study, "Fortune 500 companies lose at least $31.5 billion a year by failing to share knowledge.[42]

Underutilization: Ageism also results in the underutilization of a significant portion of the workforce. When older employees are not given opportunities to fully contribute their skills and knowledge, it directly impacts the company's overall productivity.

Knowledge transfer: When older employees become marginalized, knowledge transfer is impaired. Older employees often serve as mentors to younger staff, fostering a culture of learning and knowledge transfer. Ageism disrupts this valuable dynamic, leading to a loss of institutional knowledge and reduced skill development among younger employees.

Collaboration: Age discrimination can lead to the formation of workplace in-groups and out-groups, which reduces information shar-

41 https://www.future-work.co.uk/news/the-hidden-cost-of-ageism-a-barrier-to-innovation-and-growth/
42 https://www.learntowin.com/blog/cost-of-lost-knowledge and https://www.shrm.org/topics-tools/news/hr-magazine/shedding-light-knowledge-management

ing and collaboration across age groups. This can create silos within the organization, hampering overall productivity and innovation.

Self-fulfilling stereotypes: Negative age-related stereotypes can result in worker underperformance, even for employees who have performed strongly before. This can occur through external pressures (fear of confirming stereotypes) or internal beliefs (internalizing stereotypes), creating a vicious cycle that impacts productivity.[43]

Churn: Ageism can lead to higher turnover rates, as experienced employees leave or are forced into early retirement. This increases recruitment and training costs for companies.

Reputation: Finally, companies known for age discrimination may face reputational damage, potentially affecting their ability to attract talent and customers.

By addressing ageism and fostering an age-inclusive culture, companies can tap into the full potential of their workforce, combining the strengths of different generations to drive productivity and innovation.

Country Study: Germany

A country study for Germany provides further insights into the economic cost of ageism:

Labor market effects: According to a recent study by The Stepstone Group,[44] delaying retirement and increasing labor force participation of older workers could provide significant economic benefits to Germany:

- If more German workers chose to delay their retirements, this shift could add up to 570,000 additional workers annually to the labor market from 2030 to 2035.

---

43 https://blogs.lse.ac.uk/businessreview/2022/02/03/ageism-in-the-workplace-the-privilege-of-being-the-right-age/

44 https://www.thestepstonegroup.com/english/newsroom/press-releases/delaying-retire-ment-boost-for-the-economy-28-billion-euros-potential-per-year-for-germany/

- Increased workforce participation could boost Germany's economy by up to €28 billion per year.

Motivations and preferences: The same study found that approximately 39 percent of individuals aged 55 and older is interested in working beyond the standard retirement age. Their main motivations include:

- enjoyment of work (75 percent)
- financial security (61 percent)
- intellectual stimulation (60 percent)
- social interactions (57 percent)

On average, these workers wish to extend their careers by four years and work 24 hours per week.

Conditions for continued employment: To encourage older workers to remain in the workforce, employers should consider offering:

- flexible working hours (desired by 65 percent)
- financial incentives like bonuses or pension allowances (55 percent)
- options for part-time work or job sharing (45 percent)
- regular feedback and recognition (42 percent)
- health support (30 percent)

Economic impact: Dr. Tobias Zimmermann of The Stepstone Group emphasized that encouraging older workers to continue working under the right conditions is crucial for counteracting potential labor shortages due to demographic changes. This increased workforce participation could help maintain productivity and prosperity in the German economy.

Healthcare costs: As the German population ages, the direct healthcare costs associated with physical inactivity are projected to increase constantly until 2060.[45] Ageism can exacerbate this trend by discouraging older adults from staying physically and socially active.

---

45   https://eurapa.biomedcentral.com/articles/10.1186/s11556-017-0187-1

The highest direct per capita healthcare costs are observed in the 65+ age group, particularly for diseases like ischemic heart disease and Type 2 diabetes. Ageism in healthcare can lead to inadequate prevention and treatment, potentially increasing these costs further.

Economic growth: Germany's potential output growth is expected to slow down due to demographic changes, with median growth rates projected to remain at approximately 0.4 percent throughout the 2020s.[46] Ageism contributes to this trend by underutilizing the skills and experience of older workers.

Loss of valuable experience: A total of 11 percent of German workers over age 50 report experiencing ageism in the workplace.[47] This discrimination risks losing valuable experience from the labor market, potentially reducing productivity and innovation.

Productivity losses: Age discrimination leads to the underutilization of skills and experience of older workers, potentially reducing overall economic productivity.[48]

Social security and pension costs: Ageism can push older workers toward early retirement, increasing the strain on Germany's social security and pension systems. This effect is particularly pronounced, given Germany's aging population demographics.

Reduced workforce diversity: Ageism limits age diversity in the workplace, which can negatively impact creativity, problem-solving, and overall organizational performance.

While it's challenging to quantify the exact economic cost of ageism in Germany, these factors collectively suggest a substantial negative impact on the country's economic performance and future growth prospects. Addressing ageism could help mitigate some of the economic challenges posed by Germany's aging population.

46 https://www.sachverstaendigenrat-wirtschaft.de/fileadmin/dateiablage/Arbeitspapiere/ Arbeitspapier_02_2024.pdf

47 https://totalent.eu/discrimination-still-plagues-the-german-labour-market/

48 https://totalent.eu/discrimination-still-plagues-the-german-labour-market/

Addressing ageism is not just a matter of fairness; it's an economic imperative. As populations age and career trajectories evolve, creating inclusive work environments that support employees throughout their careers will be essential for organizational success and societal progress.

Sustainability, Innovation, and Growth

The aging workforce has significant implications for sustainability, innovation, and economic growth across many countries. This demographic shift presents both challenges and opportunities that require careful consideration and policy responses.

Impact on Economic Growth and Productivity

An aging workforce can potentially reduce labor productivity growth, primarily through its negative effect on Total Factor Productivity (TFP) growth. Projections suggest that workforce aging could reduce TFP growth by an average of 0.2 percentage point annually over the next two decades.[49] This decline in productivity growth is concerning, as it can hamper overall economic expansion.

Several factors contribute to this productivity challenge:
- concentration of older workers in occupations where productivity decreases with age
- reduced labor force participation as more workers retire
- increased healthcare and pension costs straining public finances

However, the impact is not uniformly negative. Some studies indicate that multigenerational workforces can be more productive than those comprised of primarily younger workers.[50] Leveraging the experience and skills of older workers alongside the energy of younger employees may spark innovation and knowledge transfer.

---

49 https://www.imf.org/external/pubs/ft/wp/2016/wp16238.pdf
50 https://wiseforceadvisors.com/2021/05/04/social-sustainability-and-the-aging-workforce/

Effects on Innovation and Technological Adoption

The relationship between an aging workforce and innovation is complex. Older workers may be less inclined to adopt new technologies or work processes; however, their accumulated experience and knowledge can be valuable for innovation when properly leveraged. Companies may need to invest more in retraining and upskilling older workers to keep pace with technological change. To maintain innovation in an aging society, policies supporting research and development, as well as lifelong learning initiatives, will become increasingly important.

Sustainability Challenges and Opportunities

An aging workforce intersects with sustainability goals in several ways:

- **Environmental:** Some research suggests that aging populations may lead to reduced carbon emissions by promoting industrial upgrading and shifts in consumption patterns.[51] But the overall impact on environmental sustainability continues to be debated and likely varies by context.
- **Social:** Ensuring fair treatment and opportunities for older workers is crucial for social sustainability. This includes preventing age discrimination in hiring and workplace practices, providing flexible work arrangements and phased retirement options, and ensuring equitable access to healthcare and long-term care services.
- **Economic:** Maintaining a productive workforce as the population ages is essential for economic sustainability. This may require adapting pension systems to encourage longer working lives, investing in healthcare to keep older workers healthy and productive, and supporting small and medium-sized enterprises in adapting to an aging workforce.[52]

---

51 https://www.nature.com/articles/s41599-024-02914-9
52 https://population-europe.eu/research/discussion-papers/discussion-paper-no-9-age-ing-workforce-social-cohesion-and-sustainable

Policy Implications and Strategies

To address the challenges and harness the opportunities of an aging workforce, policymakers and businesses should consider:

- investing in lifelong learning and skill development programs
- promoting age-diverse workplaces and combating age discrimination
- redesigning roles and work environments to accommodate older workers' needs
- encouraging flexible retirement policies and phased retirement options
- strengthening healthcare systems to support worker wellness across all age groups
- fostering innovation and technological adoption while leveraging older workers' experiences
- developing targeted policies to support vulnerable groups within the aging workforce

By implementing comprehensive strategies that address these areas, countries can work toward creating more sustainable, innovative, and productive economies in the face of demographic change. The key lies in viewing older workers as a valuable resource rather than a burden, and in creating systems that support their continued contribution to the workforce and society.

CHAPTER 2 SUMMARY
The impact of aging on sustainability, innovation, and growth is significant, so organizations need to have a thoughtful age management strategy in place.

Chapter 3
Wisdom's Worth: The Business Case for a Wise Organization

Introducing the Wise Organization

Leaders who focus on managing the demographic changes in their organizations don't seem to have a suitable term for this endeavor. It's a relatively new topic—and most organizations do not have a designated business function that takes responsibility for these challenges. Is it the job of human resources or talent management? Is it a people issue or a business imperative?

So far in this book, I have been using the term "age management" to describe a tactical approach that some organizations take to manage their workforces, with a specific focus on the needs and contributions of an aging population. This concept encompasses various practices aimed at enhancing the health, productivity, and job satisfaction of older employees, particularly those aged 50 and above. It's a good start, but I believe it doesn't go far enough.

I see age management as a reactive approach to a developing problem. Companies that approach the issue this way almost certainly are doing too little, too late. They won't capture the full strategic potential of managing a multigenerational workforce proactively. As you continue to read this book, you'll gain deep insight and practical advice for changing the mindset within your organization. Instead of reacting to demographic change, you'll see how to take a proactive approach that turns your aging workforce into an asset that improves productivity and competitiveness.

The EU refers to age management as the management of human resources with an explicit focus on the requirements of an aging workforce. In this interpretation, age management is holistic, intergenerational, and life-course oriented.

However, even this definition is reactive in nature. It outlines how to think about the needs of an aging workforce and suggests solutions for each need, as illustrated in the graphic below.[53]

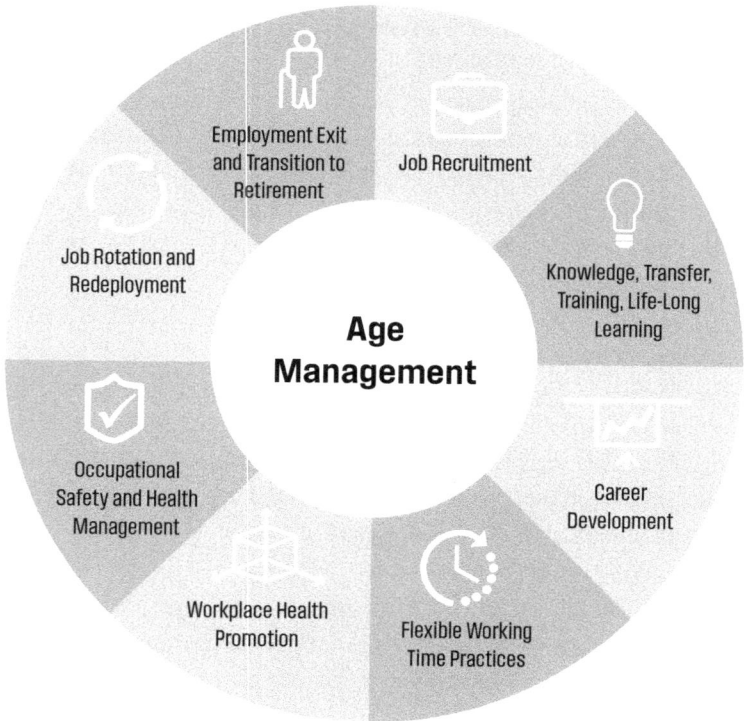

The circular diagram titled "Age Management" contains the following segments: Employment Exit and Transition to Retirement; Job Recruitment; Knowledge, Transfer, Training, Life-Long Learning; Career Development; Flexible Working Time Practices; Workplace Health Promotion; Occupational Safety and Health Management; Job Rotation and Redeployment.

53   https://eguides.osha.europa.eu/all-ages/what-age-management-0

The suggestions include how to promote workplace health to better align with the changing needs of the older employees. Or how to offer more flexible working time to better match the requirements of the aging workforce. Or how to revise training efforts to match the lingering knowledge obsolescence of the mature workers. Or how to re-think career development to promote life-long learning and careers as more and more employees are in their fifties and sixties.

Because age management focuses primarily on the needs of the aging, the closely related aspects of integration and inclusion across different age groups gets lost in translation. In response, some organizations have embraced the idea of age diversity management, hinting at a more proactive approach that considers employees from various age groups within the workplace.

What is Age Diversity Management?

A people management approach that some organizations follow to include diverse age groups in the workforce and leverage the unique strengths of each generation.

Age diversity management is not only about compliance, but it's also about harnessing the strengths of a diverse workforce. For example, a multigenerational workforce enhances decision-making and innovation by combining different viewpoints. It also helps facilitate knowledge exchange: Older employees can mentor younger ones, while younger employees can introduce new technologies and explain emerging trends.[54] On the other hand, organizations must react to and confront potential biases and communication barriers that arise from generational differences. Effective age diversity management includes creating inclusive policies that support all age groups and encourage collaboration.

---

54   https://ersj.eu/journal/2752/download/Age+Diversity+Management++Conceptu-al+and+Application+Approach.pdf and https://www.fm-magazine.com/news/2024/aug/the-role-of-managing-age-diversity-workplace/

Considering age diversity as part of broader diversity, equity, and inclusion (DEI) initiatives is vital. This includes ensuring that age-related considerations are part of recruitment, retention, and professional development strategies.

As a fiftysomething professional, I would choose to work in an organization that's focused on age diversity management over one that's simply taking tactical measures to manage older workers. However, as a leadership consultant, I see a much bigger opportunity. When leaders approach the systemic shift in age distribution strategically, they are able to change the narrative around age in their organizations and turn their aging workforces into a source of competitive advantage. In short, they become Wise Organizations. If I could choose, I'd absolutely want to work in a Wise Organization for the next chapters of my career.

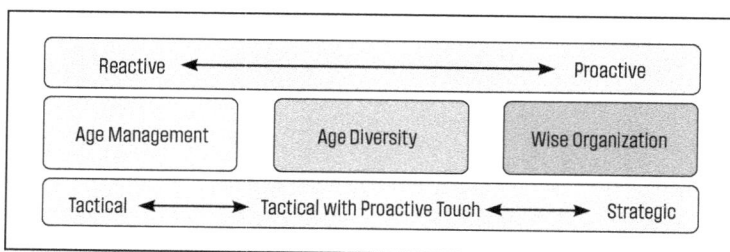

What Is a "Wise Organization"?

Over the years, I've often seen how HR managers struggle to gain executive buy-in when flagging the need to consider the changing age distribution in an organization. While there is a general awareness that an aging workforce impacts company performance, many leaders consider age-aware initiatives as a "nice-to-have." HR-driven initiatives often start with great enthusiasm, but without a broader understanding from the business, these efforts are doomed to fail.

If 30 percent of your employees are soon to be over the age of 50, age distribution will be a strategic challenge. Navigating it successfully requires a fundamental mindset change. Companies that understand this difference and embrace the shift in age distribution strategically are on their way to becoming Wise Organizations. We refer to their management approach as Wise Management.

A Wise Organization leverages the collective experience of the entire employee base to sharpen its competitive edge and execute on strategic business priorities. This approach aligns with the needs of the aging worker and facilitates intergenerational communication and teamwork to leverage the unique strengths of each age group for the benefit of the organization and the wellbeing of older individuals.

The Business Case for a Wise Organization

Companies in competitive markets face an onslaught of difficult business challenges. They must find ways to innovate and transform, while increasing productivity and navigating talent shortages. Given the macro picture of demographic change and a rapidly aging workforce, how should leaders prepare for the future?

I recommend asking these questions to begin:

- How can your current leadership approach help navigate demographic shifts in the organization?
- How well have you prepared to manage an aging workforce as it relates to corporate culture, team effectiveness, and the bottom line?

I've posed these questions to many WiseForce Advisors clients over the years, and a majority of them believe that the organizations they work for are not managing the challenges of an aging workforce sufficiently. Most of them want their organizations to take action now to address the aging trend as it unfolds. Several concerns shape this point of view, and it is from these discussions that I've concluded it's imperative to start the transformation into a Wise Organization today:

Strategic implications: The leaders I talk to are wondering how workforce demographics will impact their organizations' abilities to execute long-term strategies. They see potential risks arising, but they haven't yet formulated a response to the trend.

Talent management: HR directors tell me they are not sufficiently leveraging the experience of older employees because they seem to be stuck in an outdated age narrative. ("We'll turn to young talent to build the future.") And they recognize its importance to develop intergenerational knowledge transfer programs to preserve critical institutional knowledge.

Innovation and adaptability: In my consulting work, clients often express strongly held beliefs about how an age-diverse culture will influence their capacity to innovate and adapt to change. But they struggle to foster diverse perspectives across different age groups to drive creativity and problem-solving.

Workforce planning: In recent years, we've noticed that organizations are aware of the changing age distribution, and HR departments especially understand that a significant percentage of the current workforce is going to retire in the next few years. Despite efforts to offset this trend with workforce planning, demographic change presents an overwhelming challenge for leaders who are trying to develop a comprehensive response to retain knowledge and replace personnel in key roles.

Company culture and engagement: Many business leaders want to have better mechanisms in place to counter hidden age biases and improve engagement and productivity.

Financial considerations: Leaders often refer to progress they have been making by offering flexible work arrangements that could benefit both the company and employees financially.

Beside these factors, four more considerations support the business case for a Wise Organization:
1. the impact of demographic change on transformation initiatives
2. the impact of demographic change on sustainability agendas

3. workflow routine
4. personal change

Impact on Business Transformation

Business transformation refers to the comprehensive and strategic process of making significant changes to an organization's structure, processes, and technologies to enhance performance and competitiveness. This kind of transformation is essential for organizations to adapt to evolving market conditions, improve efficiency, and create new value. Related changes often involve some mix of people, processes, and technology.

According to KPMG's Business Digital Transformation Monitor for 2024, 27 percent of companies have a formal digital transformation strategy in place, an increase of 6 percentage points from the previous year.[55] When companies mismanage demographic changes, they also hinder transformation agendas in the following ways:

Skill gaps and knowledge loss: As older, experienced workers retire without proper knowledge transfer mechanisms in place, organizations risk losing valuable institutional knowledge and expertise. This impedes transformation efforts, as companies lack the necessary skills and insights to implement new strategies or technologies effectively.

Reduced innovation and adaptability: Failing to manage demographic changes can result in a workforce that lacks diversity in age, background, and perspective. This homogeneity can stifle innovation and creativity, which are crucial for successful transformation.[56] Without a mix of experienced professionals and younger employees with fresh ideas, companies may struggle to adapt to rapidly changing market conditions and technological advances.

55　https://kpmg.com/pl/en/home/insights/2024/06/business-digital-transformation-monitor-edition-2024.html
56　https://www.wifor.com/en/demographic-change/

Productivity challenges: Demographic shifts lead to productivity challenges when they are not managed proactively. An aging workforce may face physical limitations or require different working conditions, potentially impacting overall productivity.[57] Conversely, a predominantly younger workforce might lack the experience necessary for certain complex tasks. Failure to address these issues can slow transformation initiatives and hinder operational efficiency.

Increased recruitment and training costs: Insufficient management of demographic changes often leads to higher turnover rates and increased recruitment needs. As experienced workers retire or leave, companies may find themselves constantly hiring and training new employees, which can be costly and time-consuming.[58] These additional expenses and efforts divert resources from transformation projects, delaying their implementation or reducing their scope.

Cultural misalignment: Demographic changes often bring about shifts in workplace culture and values. Younger generations may have different expectations regarding work-life balance, career progression, and company values compared to older employees. This misalignment can create friction, reduce employee engagement, and ultimately hinder the successful implementation of transformation initiatives.

Resistance to change: Older employees may feel threatened by new technologies or ways of working, while younger employees might be frustrated by outdated processes. This resistance can derail transformation efforts, as employees may be unwilling to adopt new systems or methodologies.

Talent attraction and retention challenges: Organizations that fail to adapt to changing workforce demographics may struggle to attract and retain top talent. Younger workers often seek employers that offer flexible work arrangements, opportunities for growth, and a diverse, inclusive environment. Companies that don't meet these expec-

---

57 https://www.innerspace.eu/why-the-demographic-change-is-a-risk-for-your-production/
58 https://hbr.org/2008/02/managing-demographic-risk

tations may find it difficult to secure the talent necessary to drive their transformation agendas forward.

Reduced market competitiveness: As demographics shift, customer bases and market demands evolve as well. Companies that don't effectively manage their internal demographic changes may struggle to understand and meet the needs of their changing customer bases. This misalignment can result in reduced competitiveness, which will hinder the success of transformation initiatives aimed at improving customer experience or expanding market share.

Compliance and legal risks: Failing to address demographic changes can expose companies to compliance and legal risks. Age discrimination, for example, can become a significant issue if organizations don't have proper policies and practices in place to manage an age-diverse workforce. Such legal challenges divert attention and resources from transformation efforts and damage the company's reputation.

For all of these reasons and more, demographic changes threaten to undermine transformation efforts. Make sure you don't let this catch you by surprise. Choose instead to approach it with a Wise Organization mindset.

Impact on Sustainability Efforts

ESG (Environmental, Social, and Governance) initiatives are about measuring and improving a company's impact on the environment, society, and its own governance practices. These initiatives have become crucial in today's business landscape for several reasons:

1. **Risk management:** ESG efforts help to identify and mitigate potential risks that could significantly impact a company's reputation, profits, and operations.
2. **Investor expectations:** Two-thirds of investors now consider ESG factors in their investment decisions. Companies with strong

ESG performance are viewed as less risky and better positioned for long-term success.[59]

3. **Regulatory compliance:** There is a rapidly evolving regulatory landscape requiring companies to be more transparent about their ESG practices.[60] Stakeholder pressure: Employees, customers, and the public increasingly expect companies to act responsibly and contribute to a sustainable future.

4. **Financial performance:** ESG is now considered alongside traditional financial metrics to predict future performance and return on investment.

The stakes are high for companies implementing sustainability initiatives—particularly in the face of the demographic changes we've been talking about in this book. A corporate sustainability strategy that does not account for changing demographics is short-sighted, ineffective, and likely to fail. It is critical to incorporate demographic changes into your sustainability strategy to:

− align with the resulting shift of consumer demands
− address the risk of facing critical skill shortages as experienced workers retire, potentially resulting in a significant loss of valuable institutional knowledge and expertise and an eroding competitive advantage
− capitalize on the innovation potential of a multigenerational workforce
− adjust to and benefit from varying levels of technological proficiency

Leaders who are preparing for demographic change stand to improve their social sustainability performance, which in turn affects the entire value chain. Other elements of social sustainability certainly are important—employee wellbeing, fair pay and labor practices, commu-

---

59   https://plana.earth/academy/esg-performance
60   https://riskonnect.com/resources/esg-reporting/

nity engagement, supply chain responsibility, and corporate social responsibility. However, initiatives that do not put demographic change at the center will be limited in their potential impact.

The Routine Trap

"I've been around here long enough to know how to fix these problems, but my manager only trusts me to do the same tasks every day."

Sound familiar? Recently, I overheard an employee sharing this sentiment with a colleague in the office where I was consulting. Any way you look at it, this becomes a "lose-lose" situation. The organization loses, as it does not benefit from existing experience. And the individual loses, as the employee feels undervalued and won't contribute more than the bare minimum of what's expected of him.

A few days later, I met the unhappy worker in the cafeteria, and we started talking. I confessed that I had overheard his conversation, and he elaborated:

"I've been in this game for over three decades now, and I hit my fifties a few years back. Sure, I've got my niche. I know my stuff inside out, and I can do my job with my eyes closed. But that's part of the problem, you see?

"Every day, I walk into the office, sit at my desk, and it feels like Groundhog Day. Same tasks, same challenges, same old routine. My boss? He's happy as long as I'm ticking boxes and meeting deadlines. 'If it ain't broke, don't fix it' seems to be the motto around here.

"Now and then they send us to some training to keep us up to speed on the latest industry jargon or a new software update. But real professional growth? Forget about it.

"I look around at my colleagues, so many of us in the same boat. We're comfortable, but we're stagnating. It's like we're stuck in this routine trap. We know our roles inside out, but we're not pushing boundaries anymore. We're not growing, learning, or contributing anything new.

"And let me tell you, it's soul-crushing. I've got at least another decade of work ahead of me, maybe more. The thought of spending it just going through the motions. ... It keeps me up at night sometimes.

"The company's missing out too. All this experience, years of knowledge, and they're not tapping into it. They're not pushing us to innovate, to mentor the younger crowd, to make any kind of difference. What if they saw us as more than just reliable old workhorses? What if they gave us real opportunities to grow, to lead, to change?

"For now, here I am, stuck in my comfortable rut, watching the years tick by. It's a trap, and I'm not sure how to get out of it. At the same time, big changes make me nervous, so I'm not sure how I'd react if something new did come along. I've seen too many initiatives fail over the years."

It's easy to imagine how older workers who settle into a stagnant routine may develop a negative attitude toward change in the workplace, perceiving any deviation from the norm as a threat. A detour into the field of neuroscience helps us understand that resisting change is a normal part of human behavior as we age—and something we can work *with* instead of *against*.

The SCARF Model

When I first came across the Status, Certainty, Autonomy, Relatedness, and Fairness (SCARF) model, I was intrigued by the idea that neuroscience could help us understand behavioral patterns in social contexts at work. Developed by Dr. David Rock, co-founder and CEO of the NeuroLeadership Institute, this model uniquely blends neuroscience, with its strong ties to biology, and psychology to show how the human brain is programmed to respond to social stimuli. Humans tend to be irrational beings, driven by fear of threats and, to a lesser extent, the promise of rewards. Here is a breakdown of each pattern in the model:

- **Status**: the relative importance of an individual to others and their own sense of worth as a result

- **Certainty**: being able to predict future events with few major surprises
- **Autonomy**: being able to have control over oneself and events
- **Relatedness**: a sense of connection and safety in relation to others
- **Fairness**: a perception of a just and fair environment

When humans are in a threat state—potentially triggered by any of these stimuli—the brain sinks into a "limbic" mode, incapable of higher-order thinking or social interaction. The conscious brain exits the building, leaving your actions to the whim of the fight-or-flight response. By contrast, when you're in the reward state, your brain can be more creative, thoughtful, and collaborative.[61]

This theory can be applied in ways that support leadership and organizational development. If we understand how the human brain works through this model, we can predict and influence behavior in work settings.

In fact, I think it's critically important for leaders to understand these behavioral patterns when planning for an aging workforce. By intentionally applying the SCARF model to aging workplace scenarios, leaders can create an environment that minimizes social threats and maximizes rewards, leading to improved motivation, collaboration, and overall job satisfaction.

See below to learn more about the behavior to be expected when patterns are rewarded or threatened:

61 https://modelthinkers.com/mental-model/scarf-model

When patterns are rewarded, the behavior manifests as:	When patterns are threatened, people may exhibit the following behavior:
STATUS Status refers to our relative importance to others. People are motivated to maintain or improve their social standing. • feeling valued and respected by colleagues and superiors • recognition for achievements and contributions • opportunities for growth and advancement To support status needs, leaders can: • provide regular, constructive feedback • publicly acknowledge accomplishments • offer mentoring and development opportunities	STATUS People are threatened when it's diminished. When status is threatened, people may: • become defensive or argumentative • attempt to assert dominance or expertise • dismiss others' ideas or contributions • disengage from the conversation or task • seek validation or recognition from others
CERTAINTY Certainty relates to our ability to predict future outcomes. Humans crave predictability, clear expectations, and goals. • consistent processes and procedures • transparent communication about changes To increase certainty, organizations can: • establish clear objectives and timelines • provide regular updates on projects and company direction • create stable routines and rituals	CERTAINTY When certainty is threatened, individuals may: • resist change or new initiatives • seek excessive details or guarantees • become anxious or stressed • procrastinate on decisions or actions • spread rumors or speculate to fill information gaps

When patterns are rewarded, the behavior manifests as:	When patterns are threatened, people may exhibit the following behavior:
AUTONOMY Autonomy is about having a sense of control over one's environment and decisions. People feel rewarded when they have choices and the freedom to make decisions about how to accomplish tasks. • flexibility in work arrangements • opportunities to provide input on team or organizational decisions To promote autonomy, managers can: • delegate responsibilities and trust employees to deliver • allow flexible working hours or remote work options when possible • involve team members in decision-making processes	AUTONOMY When their autonomy is restricted, people often: • push back against directives or micromanagement • become resentful or uncooperative • seek ways to regain control, even in unrelated areas • decrease productivity or engagement • express frustration or dissatisfaction openly
RELATEDNESS Relatedness concerns our sense of connection and belonging to a group. Humans are social creatures and thrive when they feel part of a community. In the workplace, this means: • building strong relationships with colleagues • feeling part of a team or organizational culture • having opportunities for collaboration and social interaction To foster relatedness, companies can: • encourage team-building activities and social events • promote a culture of inclusivity and respect • facilitate cross-functional collaboration	RELATEDNESS When relatedness is threatened, individuals may: • isolate themselves from the group • form cliques or exclusive subgroups • become less communicative or collaborative • show decreased trust in colleagues or leadership • exhibit reduced empathy or consideration for others

When patterns are rewarded, the behavior manifests as:	When patterns are threatened, people may exhibit the following behavior:
FAIRNESS Fairness relates to our perception of just and equitable exchanges between people. Perceived unfairness can trigger strong negative reactions. In a work environment, this includes: • equal opportunities for advancement and rewards • transparent decision-making processes • consistent application of rules and policies To ensure fairness, organizations should: • implement clear and equitable performance evaluation systems • communicate openly about decision-making rationales • address perceived inequities promptly and transparently	FAIRNESS When fairness is threatened, people typically: • express anger or resentment • seek retribution or "evening the score" • disengage from work or reduce effort • challenge decisions or authority more frequently • spread negativity among colleagues

While the SCARF model applies to people of all ages, the effect of these patterns on an aging individual tends to be more pronounced. Another concept called Life Stage Theory helps us understand why:

Life Stage Theory

Life Stage Theory is a psychological concept that divides human development into distinct phases characterized by qualitative differences in behavior and experiences.[62] The most prominent theory in this category was developed by Erik Erikson, who proposed eight stages of psychosocial development spanning from infancy to late adulthood.[63]

---

62 https://en.wikipedia.org/wiki/Erikson%27s_stages_of_psychosocial_development
63 https://www.open.edu/openlearn/mod/oucontent/view.php?id=99099&section=3.3

Erikson's eight stages of psychosocial development are:[64]

1. Trust vs. mistrust (infancy, 0–1 year)
2. Autonomy vs. shame and doubt (early childhood, 1–2 years)
3. Initiative vs. guilt (preschool, 3–6 years)
4. Industry vs. inferiority (school age, 7–10 years)
5. Identity vs. role confusion (adolescence, 11–19 years)
6. Intimacy vs. isolation (young adulthood, 20–44 years)
7. Generativity vs. stagnation (middle adulthood, 45–64 years)
8. Ego integrity vs. despair (maturity, 65 and above)

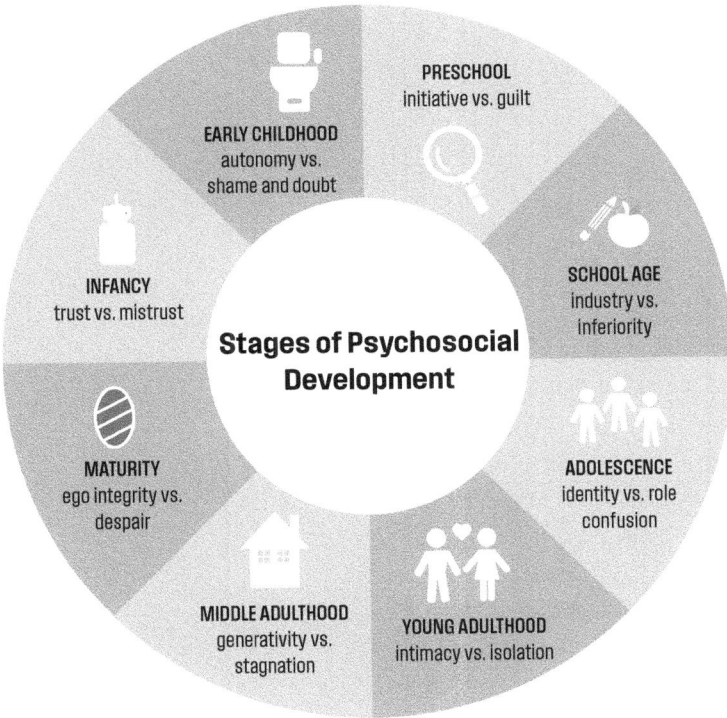

Source: https://www.verywellmind.com/erik-eriksons-stages-of-psychosocial-development-2795740

64 https://courses.lumenlearning.com/wm-lifespandevelopment/chapter/erikson-and-psy-chosocial-theory/

Each stage presents a psychosocial crisis that must be resolved, resulting in the development of specific virtues if successfully navigated. The theory suggests that unresolved conflicts from earlier stages impact later stages of development.

When I first discovered Erikson's work, I realized that the Western society I grew up in focused almost exclusively on the earlier stages of life. We talked a lot about the teenage years, but there was an assumption that once you'd reached young adulthood, you'd made it and would be OK until the inevitable mid-life crisis set in.

In the context of work, we are trained to look at the needs of younger people entering the workforce. Companies provide them with education and training, followed by functional and/or leadership education and training. But what's often overlooked is the glaring need for continued learning and support in the middle and late adulthood stages.

According to Erikson, organizations should consider five characteristics of the middle adulthood phase, which spans ages 40–65:

1. **Generativity vs. stagnation**

   Generativity involves:
   - contributing to society and future generations
   - mentoring and nurturing others
   - creating a positive legacy
   - engaging in meaningful and productive work

   Stagnation, on the other hand, may lead to:
   - self-centeredness
   - lack of growth or contribution
   - feelings of unproductiveness

2. **Midlife transitions**

   This phase often involves:
   - reevaluation of life goals and past choices
   - potential for a "midlife crisis"
   - increased focus on self-fulfillment rather than social acceptance
   - reconciling contradictions in self-identity

3. **Cognitive changes**

   Middle adulthood sees both gains and losses in cognitive abilities:
   - improved problem-solving skills based on accumulated experience
   - potential for increased creativity and wisdom
   - some decline in fluid intelligence, offset by gains in crystallized intelligence

4. **Physical changes**

   While not as dramatic as in other life stages, middle adulthood involves:
   - gradual physical changes, such as graying hair and wrinkles
   - increased focus on health and wellness
   - adaptation to bodily changes and potential health issues

5. **Social roles**

   Middle adults often find themselves in complex social situations:
   - part of the "sandwich generation," caring for both children and aging parents
   - taking on leadership roles in career and community
   - adjusting to changing family dynamics as children grow and leave home

To learn more about the source material, see the links below:[65]

Erikson's work provides insight into behavioral patterns of the aging worker. If leaders in organizations become more aware of these drivers and implications, they will be better equipped to leverage the potential of their experienced workers to achieve the corporate vision and mission. It is also vitally important to understand that aging employees, in the middle adulthood and late adulthood stages of life, adjust their goals and social preferences as they perceive their own

65 https://psychologywriting.com/middle-adulthood-development-eriksons-theory/, https://socialsci.libretexts.org/Courses/Rio_Hondo/Lifespan_Development_(Pilati)/09:_Middle_Adulthood/9.02:_Psychosocial_Development_in_Middle_Adulthood, and https://study.com/academy/lesson/physical-development-in-middle-adulthood.html

time horizons shrinking. For example, they may prioritize emotionally meaningful goals over knowledge-acquisition goals.

Laura Carstensen, Professor of Psychology and Director of the Stanford Center on Longevity, studies the role that perceived endings play in human motivation and how they impact leadership.[66] She summarized her research findings in the Socioemotional Selectivity Theory (SST).[67] In simple terms, this theory points to the fact that the aging individual becomes more selective in goal setting and pursuits. At work, this means that, unlike younger coworkers, the aging individual may not eagerly follow every initiative that leadership launches.

Susan's Story

Susan is a 60-year-old finance executive in the insurance industry who is nearing retirement. Over the years, she has become a passionate subject matter expert who frequently assumes project leadership roles. Recently, however, her coworkers observe that, instead of pursuing ambitious new projects or seeking the next promotion, Susan prioritizes mentoring younger colleagues and strengthening relationships with her team members. When she declines an opportunity to move into a people leadership role, a long-term colleague inquires about her decision-making.

Susan explains that she feels greater satisfaction in sharing her knowledge and experience, fostering a positive work environment, and leaving a lasting impact on her colleagues rather than continuing to climb the corporate ladder. She admits her focus has shifted from career advancement to more emotionally fulfilling aspects of her work. This shift in Susan's behavior aligns with Carstensen's Socioemotional Selectivity Theory in several ways:

1. **Prioritizing emotional goals:** Susan focuses on personally emotionally rewarding tasks like mentoring, which provides immediate satisfaction rather than future career benefits.

---

66   https://pmc.ncbi.nlm.nih.gov/articles/PMC8599276/
67   https://pmc.ncbi.nlm.nih.gov/articles/PMC8599276/#CIT0008

2. **Selective social interactions:** She invests more time in meaningful relationships with colleagues, potentially reducing her network size but increasing the quality of her work relationships.

3. **Positivity effect:** Susan may tend to remember and focus on positive work experiences and achievements, contributing to a more optimistic outlook on her career as she approaches retirement.

4. **Knowledge sharing:** While still valuing her expertise, Susan's motivation shifts from acquiring new skills to passing on her wisdom to the next generation of employees.

Clearly, perceived time limitations can influence an employee's goals, social preferences, and overall approach to their professional life as they near the end of their career.[68]

As time went on, Susan became a trusted mentor to colleagues who valued her knowledge and experience. But when business growth started to slow and management discontinued the mentorship program, Susan's boss directed her to focus exclusively on her core function with a strong emphasis on getting involved in the day-to-day (individual contributor) work.

Susan felt that assignment challenged her status and put her self-image as a valued colleague sharing knowledge and experience at jeopardy. Her reassigned role as an individual contributor made it difficult to continue creating value in a team. Over the next few months, Susan became defensive and withdrew from the team. Management's lack of awareness and knowledge of the bigger psychological picture led to a significant demotivation of a formerly valued employee who was known for engaging beyond her immediate role.

Selection, Optimization, and Compensation Theory

Organizations can also benefit from incorporating the 1990 research findings from Paul Baltes and Margret Baltes.[69] These researchers looked into behavioral patterns of aging individuals who select goals,

68   https://psychologyfanatic.com/socioemotional-selectivity-theory/
69   https://pmc.ncbi.nlm.nih.gov/articles/PMC8866242/

optimize their resources, and compensate for (age-related) losses to maintain functioning as they age. The Balteses summarized their findings to establish the **Selection, Optimization, and Compensation (SOC)** theory.[70] To see how this theory applies in a work context, consider the case of Peter, a 60-year-old sales professional with 35 years of experience in the field:

Selection

Peter recognizes that his energy levels aren't what they used to be, so he decides to focus on his most profitable clients and product lines. He "selects" to specialize in high-value, complex sales that require his extensive experience and expertise, rather than trying to compete with younger colleagues on high-volume, lower-value sales.

Optimization

To optimize his performance in his chosen area, Peter invests time in deepening his knowledge of the complex products he is selling. He attends specialized training sessions and seeks mentoring from senior executives to enhance his skills in negotiating large contracts.

Compensation

To compensate for reduced stamina, Peter leverages technology more effectively. He uses customer relationship management (CRM) software to track client interactions and set reminders, reducing the cognitive load of remembering every detail. He also opts for video calls instead of frequent in-person meetings to minimize travel fatigue.

By applying these SOC strategies, Peter maintains his productivity and job satisfaction while adapting to the changes that come with aging in his professional life. This approach allows him to continue being a valuable asset to his company by focusing on areas where his experience gives him a competitive edge.

---

70 https://www.frontiersin.org/journals/psychology/articles/10.3389/fpsyg.2022.832241/full

To learn more about the source material, see the links below.[71]

Peter's new boss, Stephen, welcomes the shift in attention and pro-active approach. Stephen detected the SOC pattern in Peter's behavior. At first, other sales professionals in the organization complained to Stephen that Peter was "cherry picking" deals and making isolated decisions. But with a deeper understanding of life stage changes and how to leverage the potential of an aging workforce, Stephen was able to put these discussions to rest rather quickly. Stephen also knew that allowing Peter to shift the focus to his future work contribution triggered a reward behavior in the context of the SCARF model, which further elevated Peter's motivation and energy.

The Importance of Staying in a Flow State

When I was younger, I was an active triathlete competing in long-distance races. People always asked how I was able to cope with the challenge of doing endurance sports. The answer was always the same: I just had to get to a place in my competition where I felt "in flow." Once I reached that state, the race felt easier because I felt a certain level of harmony and alignment with what I was going to do and what I felt was possible. Change, challenge, and achievement became one as I got closer to the finish line.

In his book, *Beyond Boredom and Anxiety*, Mihaly Csikszentmihalyi introduces the concept of "flow"—a state of peak enjoyment, energetic focus, and creative concentration experienced during engaging activities.[72] He examines how people can achieve this state of flow in both work and play:

71   https://pmc.ncbi.nlm.nih.gov/articles/PMC8866242/, https://www.researchgate.net/publication/281612850_Selection_Optimization_and_Compensation_at_Work_in_Relation_to_Age, and https://pmc.ncbi.nlm.nih.gov/articles/PMC4795835/

72   https://www.wiley.com/en-us/Beyond+Boredom+and+Anxiety:+Experiencing+-Flow+in+Work+and+Play,+25th+Anniversary+Edition-p-9780787951405

Csikszentmihalyi describes flow as a concentrated state in which individuals are aware of their actions but not of their awareness itself. During flow, people often lose track of time and themselves, feeling competent, in control, and in harmony with their surroundings.

In addition, certain activities provide intrinsic enjoyment, leading people to engage in them for their own sake rather than for external rewards.

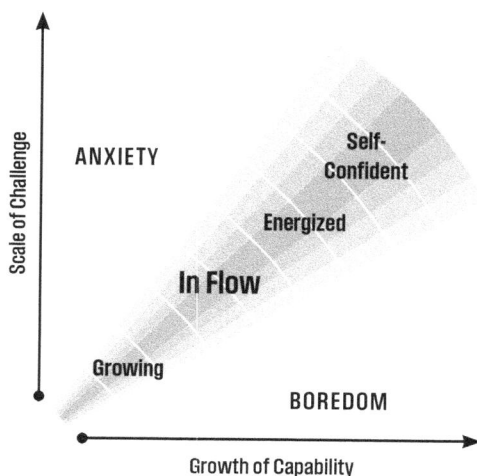

Source: Bioss 2024, adapted from original research by M. Csikszentmihalyi, 1975

What does the concept of flow look like in the context of work? People who are used to experiencing change and personal growth constantly tend to be in a flow state much of the time. As the workforce gets older, it is important to make a conscious effort to ensure that the aging individual keeps learning, changing, and growing to avoid obsolescence.

People who are not in the state of "flow" tend to experience negative effects such as boredom, anxiety, and apathy. If aging employees do not experience the flow state, their work and personal activities will reflect this stagnation through decreased performance, reduced motivation, and potential for burnout.

A persistent lack of flow experiences may even lead to decreased life satisfaction, a reduced ability to handle life's ambiguities, and the potential for turning to negative coping mechanisms such as alcoholism or family disruption.[73]

It's important to note that, while flow states are generally positive, not being in flow is a normal part of life. The key is to find a balance and create opportunities for flow experiences in various aspects of one's life. This remains the case in older age as well.

I remember a conversation with a workshop participant in which the goal was to help group members to rediscover their personal purposes in the later stage of their careers. This individual confessed that he had not felt himself in a flow state for a long time and was struggling with his current situation. He described a feeling of being stuck and alternating between two sets of emotions—sometimes bored with his routine while at the same time anxious trying out new things. During the workshop, he discovered that the first step to get out of that uncomfortable place was to find his new North Star that would lead the way. It was a catalytic moment from which the rest would flow.

In the workplace, it is important for leaders to create optimal conditions for older employees to experience the positive emotions of being in a flow state, so they don't end up feeling bored or anxious. Leaders who make a point of providing ongoing opportunities to learn and change will be able to maximize the personal growth and organizational potential of this demographic.

In light of this reality, leaders should take the looming threat of knowledge obsolescence within an aging workforce seriously. The effects may not be obvious at first, but they build up and eventually lead to a point of no return.

Imagine that the knowledge of a certain employee gets increasingly outdated (due to rapid technology advancements) and it is not sufficiently backed up by training. It will reach a point where upskilling

73 https://jyriand.com/posts/dangers-of-flow/

could even become obsolete and re-skilling presents a huge threat to the individual. So, the employee is stuck. The lack of learning experiences also prevents people from experiencing personal growth. This could impede personal and job satisfaction (due to a lack of "flow") and/or lead to layoffs.

The owner of a mid-size machine manufacturing company once told me that the organization had made a mistake by supporting a certain group of employees in becoming experts in a very narrow field. When that expertise was no longer required because of rapid technological change, this group of employees had very limited transferable skills and their ability to be re-skilled was limited. The owner is now facing a dilemma: Keep unproductive workers on the payroll or violate the loyalty of long-tenured employees by letting them go?

If left unchecked, knowledge obsolescence can have a long-term financial impact on a business in the form of reduced profitability, decreased productivity, higher labor costs, increased retirement rates, and the need for ongoing capital expenditures. Research has shown that firms experiencing higher rates of technological obsolescence tend to underperform financially compared to firms with lower obsolescence rates:[74]

Allowing employees to fall into a "routine trap" is a leadership issue that often leads to ageism and reinforces unconscious bias against older employees (see Chapter 4 on addressing stereotypes and misconceptions). To prevent these negative outcomes and avoid risking the success of strategic initiatives, companies need to provide ways for their 50+ employees to continue developing as individuals. If you take steps now to prevent the loss of productivity and the added cost of a mismanaged workforce, you'll be in a better position to win in the future.

---

74   https://www.nber.org/system/files/working_papers/w29504/w29504.pdf

The Aging Workforce Facing AI

Artificial intelligence (AI) is changing the way we work, and the effects are increasingly being felt across the entire workforce. People like to ponder what types of jobs are most likely to be eliminated by AI. Perhaps, for example, it will be white-collar workers earning up to $80,000 annually who are replaced by AI automation:[75]

1. **Clerical and administrative roles:** Data entry clerks, administrative secretaries, and bank tellers are among the most at-risk jobs.[76]

2. **Information processing jobs:** Positions in IT and other industries that heavily rely on programming and writing skills are highly exposed to AI automation.

3. **Accounting and financial roles:** These professions are predicted to face significant job losses due to AI.

These categories are not related to age and likely not to be exhaustive. The impact of AI on the aging workforce, specifically, presents both challenges and opportunities. Let's look at the opportunities first:

Older workers remain valuable in the era of AI for several reasons:[77]

1. **Experience and context:** AI cannot yet—and may never—replicate the decades of experience and contextual understanding that older workers possess. This wealth of knowledge is crucial for strategic decision-making and problem-solving.

2. **Human connection:** Older workers excel in areas where human interaction and emotional intelligence are essential, skills that AI currently lacks.

75 https://www.forbes.com/sites/ariannajohnson/2023/03/30/which-jobs-will-ai-replace-these-4-industries-will-be-heavily-impacted/

76 https://explodingtopics.com/blog/ai-replacing-jobs and https://www.weforum.org/stories/2023/05/jobs-lost-created-ai-gpt/

77 https://www.aarp.org/work/careers/automation-technology-work/, https://www.forbes.com/sites/williamarruda/2024/08/04/how-the-rise-of-the-ai-enabled-employee-will-impact-career-success/, https://www.welcometothejungle.com/en/articles/ai-and-ageism-in-the-workplace, https://www.moveworks.com/us/en/resources/blog/how-does-generative-ai-increase-productivity, and https://www.nngroup.com/articles/ai-tools-productivity-gains/

3. **Adaptability:** Contrary to stereotypes, older workers can adapt to new technologies. AI tools can augment their skills, with studies showing an up to 66 percent increase in employee productivity with generative AI.

4. **Complementary skills:** AI and older workers can work synergistically. While AI handles routine tasks, older employees can focus on strategic initiatives and creative problem-solving.

5. **Unique advantages:** AI tools can be particularly beneficial for older workers, helping them overcome physical limitations and extend their careers.

6. **Knowledge transfer:** Older workers play a crucial role in mentoring and transferring knowledge to younger colleagues, a function that AI can't replace.

7. **Diverse perspective:** Older workers contribute to a multi-generational workforce, bringing valuable insights and diversity of thought to AI implementation and usage.

In conclusion, older workers remain indispensable in the AI era, offering a unique combination of experience, adaptability, and human skills that complement and enhance AI capabilities in the workplace.

Irreplaceable: The Art of Standing Out in the Age of Artificial Intelligence

AI and automation expert Pascal Bornet explores the reality of our AI-driven world in this new book, stating that the challenges of critical thinking are becoming increasingly subtle and complex.[78]

He identifies three levels where critical thinking becomes essential in dealing with AI systems. First, the basic validation of outputs—checking for obvious errors or inconsistencies. Second, understanding the context and limitations of AI-generated responses. Third, and most crucial, examining the underlying assumptions and implications of AI

---

78 https://www.linkedin.com/in/pascalbornet/

systems. One does not have to be an AI expert to do this. It is about understanding who built the model and what biases might be embedded. *Irreplaceable* calls for a synergistic approach to critical thinking. This means leveraging AI's capabilities while maintaining and strengthening our uniquely human abilities to question, analyze, and judge. It's not about choosing between human thinking and artificial intelligence, but about creating a more powerful combination of both. That said, experience, wisdom and institutional knowledge will play a key role—all of which are associated with the mature workforce.

At the same time, older workers will face unique challenges as AI advances:[79]

1. **Increased vulnerability:** Older workers are at a higher risk of exposure to AI-related job threats across job hierarchies in the EU and the US. They may be more vulnerable to redundancies due to slower adaptation to new practices and automation of work.

2. **Age-related bias:** AI systems used in recruitment processes may unintentionally perpetuate age-related discrimination, potentially eliminating older workers from candidate pools.

3. **Skills gap concerns:** Nearly three-quarters of older workers are worried about the implications of AI on the hiring process. Many feel unprepared for AI-driven workplaces, with 81 percent reporting their employers have not discussed AI-related changes with them.

However, given the unprecedented dynamic of AI and its likely impact on the way we work and interact, a great deal of uncertainty remains. AI has the potential to augment human capabilities significantly, including capabilities of the aging workforce, but we don't know exact-

79 https://www.ageing.ox.ac.uk/blog/Are-Older-Workers-Ready-for-an-AI-Takeover-at-Work and https://www.employmentlawreview.co.uk/uks-older-generation-at-risk-of-losing-jobs-to-ai/

ly how this will play out. Also uncertain is the pace of these complex developments. And this rate will be a critical driver of occupational transitions.

For all of these reasons, organizations need to embrace a new approach toward people development with unprecedented intensity on continued tech upskilling. This will also be front and center for aging workers, as they need to stay employable to fund their longer lives. At the same time, organizations need to secure a sufficient workforce as part of their longevity strategies.

Seven Ways that Wise Organizations Drive Innovation and Growth

Leveraging diverse expertise: A Wise Management approach allows companies to harness the full potential of a multi-generational workforce. Older employees bring valuable experience, wisdom, and stability to the workplace, while younger workers often generate new ideas and innovative thinking. By promoting collaboration between different age groups, organizations can benefit from a diverse range of perspectives, leading to enhanced problem-solving and innovation.

Knowledge transfer and continuity: As older employees approach retirement, companies face the challenge of knowledge transfer and potential loss of critical expertise. An effective strategy ensures smooth succession planning and knowledge sharing between generations. This continuity is essential for maintaining organizational competitiveness and fostering innovation based on accumulated wisdom.

Adapting to demographic changes: Wise Organizations proactively address the challenges posed by demographic shifts, such as potential skill shortages and the need to retain experienced workers. By implementing flexible retirement options and age-inclusive hiring practices, companies can maintain a dynamic and skilled workforce.

Improving organizational performance: Effective Wise Management strategies increase productivity, improve work quality, and create companies that are more adaptable to change. By investing in the skills and health of an aging workforce, organizations can benefit from cost containment and increased market share.

Fostering intergenerational learning: Promote intergenerational learning and knowledge transfer. This exchange of skills and perspectives between younger and older workers can lead to innovative solutions and improved organizational performance. It also helps create a more inclusive and collaborative work environment.

Addressing skills gaps: Some industries face a shortage of younger workers with necessary skills. Wise strategies can help organizations involve older workers in organizational restructuring or development, ensuring that companies retain and transfer critical skills.

Enhancing market responsiveness: An age-diverse workforce can better respond to the needs of an increasingly diverse customer base. In sectors with an aging customer base, or those supplying age-specific products or services, older employees may be particularly well-positioned to understand and meet consumer expectations. Learn more about the source material at the links below.[80]

CHAPTER 3 SUMMARY

For the foreseeable future, business success will depend on managing the aging workforce strategically. A Wise Organization leverages each generation's strengths to ensure long-term success and drive innovation in dynamic markets. By recognizing the value of workers in all age brackets, leaders create a more resilient, innovative, and competitive workforce.

80   https://www.cfr-group.com/age-management-or-how-to-benefit-from-aging-generation/, https://jemi.edu.pl/vol-8-issue-4-2012/age-management-as-a-tool-for-the-demographic-de-cline-in-the-21st-century-an-overview-of-its-characteristics, and https://www.eurofound.europa.eu/system/files/2016-01/ef05137en_1.pdf

Part Two:

Rethinking
Gray Matter

Chapter 4
Old Dogs, New Tricks: Debunking Myths About Older Workers

Perhaps you know someone like Carol, a 58-year-old software engineer with more than three decades of experience who prides herself on staying current with the latest tech and development strategies: One morning, Carol's team gathers for a weekly meeting to discuss an upcoming project involving an ambitious AI integration. Andrew, the project lead, is outlining the requirements, and Carol, who has done some research already, raises a hand, eager to contribute her ideas.

Andrew acknowledges her with a polite smile but quickly moves on. "Let's get some fresh perspectives circulating on this one," he says, scanning the conference room for a response from the younger members of the team. "Who wants to take point on the initial design?"

Carol feels a twinge of disappointment as she watches her colleagues volunteer. Throughout the meeting, her attempts to offer input are met with cursory nods before the conversation shifts back to the ideas proposed by her junior teammates.

A few weeks go by, and Carol finds herself increasingly sidelined. "Why?", Carol wondered; her performance has remained unchanged, meeting all the requirements. Earlier that year, she'd been included in brainstorming sessions for new projects and her peers had liked her ideas, but now she's no longer invited as often, and the team ignores or dismisses her suggestions with comments like, "We're looking for innovative approaches." Why had these colleagues started treating her differently all of a sudden when there had been no change in her performance or enthusiasm for the job?

Andrew's assumption that aging necessarily means a decline in innovation illustrates one of the many stereotypes that lead to systemic ageism—a form of discrimination that involves stereotypes, prejudice, and discriminatory practices targeting individuals or groups because of their age. Whether we realize it or not, these preconceived notions impact employment decisions, career trajectories, and the overall work environment for older employees. In her well-known book *This Chair Rocks* and the 2017 TED Talk "Let's End Ageism" author and activist Ashton Applewhite says that ageism is a prejudice against our future selves.[1] We all are on a path to become "old" one day, and the idea that aging is inherently negative—and the assumption that every individual ages in the same way is simply wrongheaded. "There is no line in the sand between old and young, after which it's downhill," Applewhite says.

Here, we take a more detailed look into the negative stereotypes about mature workers that persist in the workplace, exploring the multifaceted nature of these stereotypes, their origins, and their effects on both individuals and organizations:

1. **Reduced competence:** a widespread belief that older workers are less competent, particularly in cognitive tasks[2]
2. **Resistance to change:** the notion that mature employees are less adaptable and more resistant to new ideas or technologies[3]
3. **Decreased motivation:** an assumption that older workers are less motivated in their jobs
4. **Lower trainability:** the perception that mature employees are less willing to participate in training and career development
5. **Health concerns:** Beliefs about older workers being less healthy and more prone to work-family imbalance

It's important to note that not all stereotypes are negative. Some positive stereotypes about older workers include reliability and experience. Older workers are often viewed as more dependable, especially in sectors like retail and healthcare. Mature employees are frequently valued

1   https://www.ted.com/talks/ashton_applewhite_let_s_end_ageism
2   https://www.ncbi.nlm.nih.gov/books/NBK588538/
3   https://link.springer.com/doi/10.1007/978-981-287-082-7_30

for their accumulated knowledge and expertise although they may not have the assumed knowledge or expertise.

Stereotypes about aging are deeply ingrained in many cultures, affecting how older workers perceive themselves and how others view them. The prevalence and nature of stereotypes vary based on organizational characteristics, including company size and industry type. Smaller companies tend to view older workers more positively than larger corporations. Moreover, sectors that value experience and knowledge, such as craftsmanship, often hold more positive views of mature workers.

Stereotypes can have profound effects on mature workers. For example, when age is made salient, older employees may underperform due to anxiety about confirming negative stereotypes.[4] Over time, mature workers may internalize and apply age stereotypes to themselves, affecting their self-perception and performance.

Negative stereotypes can hinder the career advancement of older workers through biased evaluations and limited opportunities. Supervisors may unconsciously rate older workers lower, particularly in non-professional roles, while misconceptions about trainability and adaptability may lead to fewer development opportunities for mature employees.

Recent research challenges many of these common stereotypes: For example, a meta-analysis of 418 studies found little support for most negative stereotypes about older workers, except for reduced willingness to participate in training. Objective measures have shown that older workers are often more productive than their younger counterparts.

When companies recognize the value of mature workers, they are able to reduce early retirement and enhance organizational performance.[5]

---

4   https://www.jstor.org/stable/26157421
5   https://www.researchgate.net/publication/313125210_Age_Stereotypes_in_the_Workplace

Stereotypes and misconceptions about mature workers present a complex challenge in today's multigenerational workplace. By understanding the nature, origins, and impacts of these stereotypes, organizations can develop strategies to create more inclusive environments that value the contributions of workers across all age groups.

Ageism and the Digital Divide

When Mark walked into his office at a large enterprise software company on his 38th birthday, his colleagues greeted him with smiles and joked, "You're over the hill, now," implying that he was getting too old for the job as a coder. Mark was confronted with the harsh reality of an age-based stereotype in the fast-paced software industry that had nurtured his curiosity and energized him with professional growth, satisfaction, and fulfillment over the length of his career. He didn't feel the least bit "old."

But instead of enjoying his birthday, Mark reflected on the uncomfortable truth that his company had long favored younger employees, believing they are more adaptable to rapidly changing technologies. This bias was marginalizing older professionals within the company—and Mark's colleagues seemed to think he was about to join the ranks of this undervalued part of the workforce.

Mark remembered how experienced talent helped his organization a few years back, when the firm faced a critical challenge implementing a new internal IT system intended to bring efficiency to the business. The project, initially estimated to take six months, encountered numerous setbacks and delays. After a year of struggles, the company realized that the young team assigned to the task lacked the comprehensive understanding of the organization's complex legacy systems, which were crucial for a smooth transition.

The company had overlooked the expertise of several senior IT professionals in their forties and fifties who had intimate knowledge of these systems. As a result, they had to extend the project timeline, hire external consultants, and delay the launch of several key products.

As we can see from Mark's example, a growing "physical-digital divide" often excludes older adults from both the development and use of new technologies,[6] even when they have valuable skills and perspectives to contribute. This exclusion can lead to social isolation from younger, more digitally-connected generations and forced withdrawal from increasingly digitalized labor markets, which only reinforces ageist stereotypes about older adults' technological competence.

When Mark went home that day, he felt discouraged, yet resolved to watch out for stereotypes and prejudices at work. He concluded this kind of behavior is deceiving and potentially costly, and he wanted to do something about it.

The Value of Experience and Institutional Knowledge

In today's rapidly evolving business landscape, the experience and institutional knowledge of mature workers have become invaluable assets for organizations seeking to maintain a competitive edge. This section explores the tangible benefits of retaining and leveraging older employees, presenting quantifiable results, impact, and return on investment (ROI) that underscore their importance in the modern workforce.

The Age-Performance Paradox

Despite prevalent stereotypes, research consistently demonstrates that older workers are highly valuable to their employers. A study by Generation and the Organization for Economic Co-operation and Development (OECD) revealed a striking paradox: While 89 percent of employers reported that their midcareer and older workers performed as well as or better than younger hires, there was a significant bias against hiring candidates aged 45–64 for entry- or intermediate-level roles.[7]

---

6   https://academic.oup.com/gerontologist/article/62/7/947/6511948?login=false
7   https://www.hrdive.com/news/employers-overlook-older-applicants/696268/

This disconnect highlights a critical oversight in many hiring practices, as companies may be missing out on a wealth of talent and experience by undervaluing older job seekers.

One of the most significant advantages of employing mature workers is their tendency to remain with an organization for longer periods. According to the US Bureau of Labor Statistics, the median tenure of workers aged 55–64 across all industries was 10.4 years in 2014, more than triple the 3.0 years for workers aged 25–34.[8] This increased stability translates to:

— reduced turnover costs
— preservation of institutional knowledge
— continuity in client relationships

Productivity and Performance

Contrary to common misconceptions, older workers often outperform their younger counterparts in various ways. For example, 83 percent of employers reported that workers over 45 learn as quickly or more quickly than younger hires. And mixed-age teams have been shown to be more productive than teams of workers of the same age.

The Economic Impact of Mature Workers

Older workers make a substantial contribution to the global economy every year. In 2020, workers aged 45 and above contributed approximately $45 trillion to the worldwide economy or 34 percent of the global GDP.[9] This figure underscores the significant role mature workers play in driving economic growth and productivity.

---

8   https://www.publichealth.columbia.edu/research/others/age-smart-employer/resources/
    guides/advantages-older-workers
9   https://www.aarp.org/pri/topics/work-finances-retirement/employers-workforce/val-
    ue-of-older-workers-breaking-barriers-embracing-experience/

ROI of Investing in Mature Workers

Investing in the retention and development of mature workers can yield impressive returns for organizations. Consider these three ways of measuring the return on investment:[10]

1. **Enhanced customer relations:** Long-tenured employees often have established relationships with clients, leading to higher customer satisfaction and loyalty.

2. **Knowledge transfer:** Mature workers serve as valuable mentors, facilitating the transfer of critical skills and knowledge to younger employees. Internal knowledge sharing can reduce external training expenses significantly.

3. **Diversity of thought:** Age diversity in the workforce brings a variety of perspectives, leading to more innovative solutions and a broader understanding of the market.

The experience and institutional knowledge of mature workers represent a significant, often underutilized resource for organizations. By recognizing and leveraging the unique strengths of older employees, companies can enhance their productivity, innovation, and overall performance. The quantifiable benefits and substantial ROI associated with retaining and developing mature workers make a compelling case for age-inclusive workforce strategies (see Chapter 7). As the global workforce continues to age, organizations that embrace the value of experience will be better positioned to thrive in an increasingly competitive business environment.

Here is the story of what happened in one life-sciences company that we'll call, LifeCo:

In an effort to meet future challenges and drive the firm's overall strategy, LifeCo's leadership team adopted six guiding principles called the "Keep Changing Agenda." These principles were intended to permeate all aspects of the company's operations, contributing to

---

10   https://peopleplus.co.uk/newsitem/the-value-of-experience-why-retaining-your-older-workforce-is-crucial

its long-term success and adaptability in the dynamic life sciences industry.

The six principles address innovation, growth, sustainability leadership, operational excellence, talent development and retention, and shaping a corporate culture that fosters curiosity. The C-suite prioritized this agenda for any business initiative or discussion, and the CEO posed this question often: "How does what we're discussing align with our guiding principles?"

When LifeCo's HR leaders started to review their existing programs, they found the company's talent development focused heavily on people under 45 years of age. They also realized that, to honor all six guiding principles, they would need to include all LifeCo employees in these programs, irrespective of age. Next, they discussed what talent development could look like for the 50+ segment of employees.

The outcome was a blended learning concept that combined self-reflection and self-discovery into a journey that enables older workers to make an active and sustainable contribution to LifeCo's strategy execution. In this way, LifeCo was able to leverage the knowledge and experience of its older workers to drive the company's strategic agenda, while elevating engagement and retention of the senior workforce.

As a positive side effect of the discovery journey, LifeCo had allowed its 50+ participants to follow a self-determined approach toward their individual needs and preferences in the later stages of their careers.

Health and Productivity of Mature Employees

As the workforce ages globally, understanding and optimizing the health and productivity of mature employees have become increasingly important. This section explores the complex relationship between aging, health, and workplace productivity, as well as strategies to support and enhance the contributions of older workers.

Contrary to common stereotypes, research indicates that age alone is not a reliable predictor of workplace productivity, particularly in the service sector.[11] Cross-sectional analyses of multiple studies have found no significant relationship between age and job productivity.[12] This surprising finding can be explained by the compensatory effect of job-specific knowledge and skills that older workers accumulate over time, which can offset age-related declines in general cognitive abilities.

Several key points emerge from the research:[13]

— There is no significant variation in productivity across age groups in service sectors.
— In some cases, younger age groups may exhibit lower productivity compared to older workers (soft skills such as communication, co-ordination, or interpersonal skills). Productivity may even improve for workers aged 60-65 in certain contexts when leveraging experience based on higher education.

These findings challenge the assumption that older workers are inherently less productive, and highlight the value of experience and expertise gained over a long career.

Health Factors Affecting Productivity

While age itself may not directly impact productivity, health-related factors can play a significant role in the work performance of mature employees. As workers age, they may face increased risk of chronic health conditions and physical limitations. However, the impact on productivity is not uniform. Older workers who maintain a healthy lifestyle often contribute more to workplace productivity. And jobs that offer opportunities to stay active can help improve the health status of older employees.

11 https://www.ncbi.nlm.nih.gov/pmc/articles/PMC9405377/
12 https://www.ncbi.nlm.nih.gov/books/NBK207720/
13 https://www.ncbi.nlm.nih.gov/pmc/articles/PMC9405377/

Work-related stress can affect the mental health of employees of all ages, but mature workers may face unique challenges. For example, age-related changes in stress resilience and coping mechanisms can impact productivity. Older workers may also experience stress related to technological changes or perceived age discrimination.

Interestingly, the a.m. research shows that older workers tend to have fewer absences, both voluntary and involuntary, compared to younger workers. This increased reliability can positively impact overall productivity.

Several key factors influence the productivity of mature employees:

1. **Task type**: Allocating work related to communication and coordination to older workers can significantly enhance their productivity compared to general tasks.

2. **Employment type:** Part-time employment tends to generate higher-level productivity for older individuals compared to full-time employment.

3. **Education:** The level of education plays a role in determining productivity among older workers.

4. **Financial status**: Workers' financial situations can impact their productivity, with financial stress potentially leading to decreased work performance.

5. **Work design:** Adapting work processes and environments to accommodate age-related changes can help maintain or improve productivity.[14]

In short, the health and productivity of mature employees are critical considerations for organizations in an aging workforce. By challenging age-related stereotypes, understanding the complex factors influencing productivity, and implementing supportive strategies, employers can harness the valuable contributions of older workers while promoting their health and wellbeing. As the workforce continues to

---

14   https://academic.oup.com/policy-press-scholarship-online/book/29553/chapter-abstract/248628602?redirectedFrom=fulltext

age, organizations that successfully engage and support their mature employees will be better positioned for success in an increasingly competitive global economy.

Research on Sustained Productivity with Age

Research on age and productivity has yielded nuanced findings that challenge simplistic stereotypes about older workers. While some studies show declines in certain abilities, others reveal sustained or even improved performance with age in many domains.

Research suggests that cognitive abilities show varied trajectories with age.[15] "Fluid" cognitive abilities like processing speed and solving novel problems tend to decline from middle adulthood. "Crystallized" abilities based on accumulated knowledge and experience often remain stable or improve into older ages. And verbal abilities and tacit knowledge used in everyday problem-solving are particularly resilient to age-related declines.

Job performance depends on the specific cognitive demands, so tasks relying heavily on speed, learning new skills, and solving unfamiliar problems may see more age-related declines. Meanwhile, jobs emphasizing experience, verbal abilities, and familiar problem-solving often show sustained productivity in older workers.

Experience can offset potential cognitive declines, too: Researchers have seen that job-specific experience improves productivity for several years, with benefits plateauing after about 3.8 years in one study of manufacturing workers.[16] Managers and professionals in fields like law, medicine, and engineering often maintain high productivity into older ages due to accumulated expertise.

---

15 https://www.ageing.ox.ac.uk/download/47
16 https://www.demogr.mpg.de/papers/working/wp-2003-028.pdf

Meta-analyses and large-scale studies reveal complex patterns. Individual productivity tends to increase in early career years, stabilize in mid-career, and often decline modestly in later years.[17] The onset and steepness of any decline vary widely based on job type and individual factors. Some studies find productivity peaks in the thirties and forties for fields like research and innovation. Other analyses show relatively stable productivity across age groups, especially when considering factors beyond core task performance.[18]

Sector and Job Type Differences

Productivity patterns vary across industries and occupations. High-complexity jobs often show more positive age-productivity relationships than low-complexity jobs. Some studies find stronger negative age effects in manufacturing compared to services, though results are mixed.[19] Occupations emphasizing accumulated knowledge and experience (e.g., managers, lawyers) tend to have flatter or more positive age-productivity curves.

Research findings also contradict common age stereotypes. For instance, older workers often excel in job-relevant domains like organizational citizenship behaviors and safety practices. Age diversity in teams can enhance overall productivity by combining complementary strengths of different age groups.[20] And continuous learning and training can help maintain and even improve cognitive abilities and job performance at older ages.

These nuanced research findings have several important implications for companies that aim to create a Wise Organization:

- **Avoid age discrimination:** Blanket assumptions about declining productivity with age are not supported by evidence.

17 https://www.ageing.ox.ac.uk/download/47
18 https://academic.oup.com/workar/article/8/2/208/6574297
19 https://ftp.zew.de/pub/zew-docs/dp/dp11058.pdf
20 https://pmc.ncbi.nlm.nih.gov/articles/PMC9915412/

- **Leverage diverse strengths:** Recognize the unique contributions of workers across the age spectrum.
- **Provide targeted support:** Offer training and job design modifications to address specific age-related changes in abilities.
- **Promote lifelong learning**: Encourage ongoing skill development to maintain cognitive flexibility and job-relevant knowledge.
- **Foster intergenerational collaboration:** Create opportunities for knowledge transfer and mentoring across age groups.

CHAPTER 4 SUMMARY

If you want to unlock the potential of an aging workforce, start by challenging simplistic aging stereotypes and embracing evidence-based practices. Unfortunately, myths and stereotypes persist, and they can be deeply rooted in organizational and/or societal mindsets. This makes it more difficult to find and address, but research is pointing to an attractive upside: a productivity reserve that is ready to be discovered.

Chapter 5
The Folly of False Solutions: When Age Management Goes Wrong

Martha, the VP of Human Resources, started a routine HR leadership meeting with an important agenda topic: "I'm hearing that our 50+ workforce has unique needs. We have to do something in response to show we care." From the outside looking in, the discussion that followed demonstrated an exceptionally caring culture: "We cannot focus on the younger generation all the time; we need a better balance," one team member said. "Our mature workers want more flexibility," said another, who added, "Let's expand our health and safety policy and provide more health benefits for this group." The leadership team felt sure of their intentions and convinced they were doing the right thing. But do you see what's wrong with this approach? It reflects reactive, shortsighted measures instead of a strategic change in the overall business plan.

In this chapter, we're going to review all the ways that age management fails to create competitive advantage, so you can avoid the most common pitfalls in your own organization. The first reason, as you saw above, is a reactive approach that completely lacks business strategy. But there are other causes, too: Unclear accountability, framing age management as a diversity-only initiative, and simply asking older workers what they need are examples of age management tactics that generally fail to generate long-term productivity gains from the workforce. We'll consider these scenarios one by one, but first, a quick look at the data showing how many companies are actually even attempting to do something about their aging workforces.

Shifting the Focus to Age

Current research (representative for the Netherlands) indicates a significant shift in the approach to age management between 2009 and 2017.[21] In 2009, 47 percent of organizations offered no age management practices and 21 percent of organizations primarily implemented exit-focused strategies for managing their aging workforces. Only 19 percent of organizations had active age management strategies in place at that time.

By 2017, the percentage of organizations with no age management practices had decreased to 30 percent. Those focusing solely on exit measures dropped to just 6 percent, and the number of organizations with active age management strategies increased dramatically to 52 percent; "active" defined as measures to activate and develop.

This data shows a major positive shift over the eight-year period, with a substantial increase in the number of companies implementing proactive age management strategies. The research indicates that age management has become much more widespread and is no longer concentrated in large organizations, but has become a standard human resources practice across the economy. It's worth noting, however, that even in 2017, about 30 percent of organizations still had no formal age management practices in place, indicating there is still room for improvement.

While we don't have exact figures for 2024, the trend suggests that the percentage of companies with age management strategies has likely continued to increase in the last seven years. We know anecdotally that more companies are becoming aware of these demographic changes and the need to adapt to an aging workforce.

Despite this positive trend, as of 2020, an AARP global employer survey found that fewer than 4 percent of firms were committed to programs integrating older workers into their talent systems, with only

---

21   https://pmc.ncbi.nlm.nih.gov/articles/PMC7681210/:

an additional 27 percent saying they were "very likely" to explore this path in the future.[22]

Given these trends and the increasing importance of managing an aging workforce, it's reasonable to assume that, by 2024, the percentage of companies with age management strategies in place had likely increased further from the 52 percent reported in 2017. The question is whether these activities are part of a bigger, integrated plan—and how these companies are thinking about building and managing an intergenerational workforce.

Age Management Problem #1: Lack of Strategy

Tom and Andrea, both working in nonoperational senior HR roles in the headquarters of a $10-billion pharmaceutical company, agreed they had to come to terms with the shifting demographics in their company. Tom prepared a heatmap for the firm's core countries, illustrating the potential losses over the next few years, as many workers reach their retirement ages.

The company also had been offering attractive early retirement packages in the past, further diminishing the workforce. Tom and Andrea looked at these numbers with growing concern and decided to send out a questionnaire to 5,000 employees, whom they believed most likely to leave the firm in the foreseeable future. The HR leaders wanted to find out whether some of the mature workers in this cohort would consider working until they reached retirement age, or even beyond.

This questionnaire represented the first time the organization had launched a wider initiative concerning its mature workforce. Tom and Andrea were overwhelmed by an 80 percent response rate. Workers in a variety of roles and skill levels were indeed interested in working longer, if part-time options and other job flexibility arrangements were offered.

---

22   https://www.bain.com/insights/better-with-age-the-rising-importance-of-older-workers/

What is wrong with this picture? Again, by focusing the very first initiative on the remaining working time, the organization framed its age management effort narrowly. Setting the tone this way makes it difficult to link age management to business needs and realize the full potential of a Wise Organization. Albeit with good intentions, this management team may have set expectations for job flexibility impossibly high. Even worse, the situation enforced a sense of entitlement. As a consequence, Tom and Andrea had to spend extra time level-setting expectations and framing age management as an effort that serves both the individual and the organization.

If you want to succeed in the long term with an age management initiative, you need to frame the agenda thoughtfully and consider it from all angles before you rush to put new policies in place. As with any strategic initiative, careful planning will generate the highest returns. If Wise Management initiatives are not specifically anchored in the corporate and people strategies, the impact will be compromised. It will be seen as an isolated initiative that leaders fail to support—a "nice-to-have" that easily gets pushed to the back burner.

Age Management Problem #2: The 'What Do You Need' List

Recently, I saw the German country head of HR of a French insurance company proudly share the outcome of an initiative to determine how work-life balance could be improved for the company's aging workforce. On social media, she explained that she wanted to find out what energizes and retains the 50+ workforce, so she had assigned a team to conduct "what do you need" interviews. The results she presented centered on a few key topics:

- Support employees' care needs for older relatives, including more flexible work arrangements.
- Provide more time off for personal health checkups.
- Create a credit account system for overtime work to allow early retirement more flexibly.

- Foster community via a company network for the mature workforce.
- Provide interventions with employees and managers to create awareness of issues that arise in connection with aging.

Most commenters on the post regarded the effort positively, but I see much that is wrong with this picture. For starters, the organization has approached a complex problem by simply extending a list of fringe benefits. How will changing these policies leverage the wisdom and experience of the 50+ worker?

Companies that address age management with a "what do you need" list inevitably miss out on a huge opportunity to drive competitive advantage. If you want to leverage the unique experience and knowledge of this growing segment of the workforce, you need to provide real employability and new career opportunities, through ongoing training and development. Unless these mature workers feel the true value of their own experience, the simple list of needs—and the entire endeavor—will be pointless. Just because you've asked and checked all the boxes on the wish list, doesn't mean age management is done.

Age Management Problem #3: Fuzzy Accountability

Since the concept of age management is so new, and business management education does not address the subject, you won't find a "head of age management" in the company org. chart, or even a person whose job title clearly points to this field. This reality leaves many questions unanswered. Who exactly is responsible and accountable for successful management of the aging workforce?

In my work, I see responsibility distributed across multiple levels and roles. Senior executives and business leaders are responsible for setting the tone and strategy for company-level efforts to manage their aging workforces. The C-suite is accountable for developing and implementing age-inclusive policies and practices as part of the organization's overall human resources strategy. This includes overall sponsorship, and allocating resources and budget for strategic initiatives.[23]

Human Resources plays a central operational role in executing Wise Management practices. The HR department designs and implements specific policies and programs, and ensures fair recruitment, training, career development, and retirement transition processes for employees of all ages.

Direct supervisors have day-to-day responsibility for applying age management practices fairly within their teams. They also must be accountable for fostering an inclusive work environment and addressing any age-related issues that arise.[24]

Finally, individual employees must take ownership of their own career development and skill-building to maintain employability. And they should be held accountable for contributing to an age-inclusive workplace culture.

Several other stakeholders outside the organization play supporting roles: Policymakers need to create supportive legislative frameworks. Social partners (e.g., unions) can help shape age management policies through collective bargaining. And occupational health professionals can support health promotion initiatives for aging workers.

As you can see, effective Wise Management requires a holistic approach that should be integrated into corporate social responsibility practices. In this way, responsibility is shared across the organization, with accountability at multiple levels. Success depends on fostering intergenerational solidarity and addressing prejudices against older workers.[25]

---

23 https://msed.vse.cz/msed_2015/article/55-Nemec-Otakar-paper.pdf
24 https://www.eurofound.europa.eu/system/files/2016-01/ef05137en_1.pdf
25 https://msed.vse.cz/msed_2015/article/55-Nemec-Otakar-paper.pdf

Age Management Problem #4: Narrow Focus, Limited Reach

Some organizations make the mistake of implementing isolated measures without a comprehensive Wise Management strategy. For example, they may focus only on a limited initiative, such as abolishing age limits in recruitment ads, without altering the company's overall approach to age management.[26] Other organizations implement small-scale changes in response to specific problems without recognizing the limitations of stopgap actions or potential conflicts with existing practices.

Many people underestimate the complexity of managing an aging workforce proactively. Different stakeholders may "jump" on certain elements to address the topic quickly instead of approaching it more holistically. You can tell it's a narrow focus when lower levels of the organization get involved. Through our work at WiseForce Advisors, we've seen cases where age management gets handed down from the Chief Human Resources officer (CHRO) of a large corporation to an individual contributor in an HR department. These delegates lacked the knowledge, exposure, and budget to lead a successful initiative.

In some cases, the initial steps taken toward building a Wise Management system for the company are quickly hijacked by the organization's Diversity & Inclusion group because they may see age to be a matter of representation. This narrow focus and lack of broader understanding for building and embracing a Wise workforce inevitably leads to failed initiatives.

If senior management neglects to set the tone and strategy for age management priorities, the topic usually emerges in the People and Culture function (formerly known as HR). The outcome of an HR-led age management effort will depend on the individual who starts shaping the agenda. That person may not have a bigger understanding of the entire scope of the issue and will focus on an area they know

---

26   https://edz.bib.uni-mannheim.de/www-edz/pdf/ef/98/ef9865en.pdf

best, such as talent management or DEI. When age management remains primarily a matter of people development or simply an updated employer branding, it falls short of the potential for driving productivity gains across the enterprise.

Age Management Problem #5: Outdated Company Culture

Here's another scenario that may unfold: A textile machinery company I know well employs about 4,500 people. Leadership had tasked HR with modernizing the organization's policies and processes. The SVP of HR believed the aging workforce was causing a productivity and engagement problem. In order to address the problem, HR factored age management into its talent management processes. Managers were asked to "cover" the needs of their 50+ employees in the annual performance review process. In addition, the company decided to review and extend the people development offerings for its mature workforce.

This effort failed, predictably, because most of the company's leaders lacked a broader understanding of the aging workforce dynamic. In addition, the leadership team had internalized outdated age stereotypes, such as the idea that "we don't need to invest in older people." Moreover, the extended development initiative for the aging workforce was not linked to the company's fundamental business needs.

What had begun as a well-intentioned effort at the textile machinery company ended in disappointment for everyone involved. Within the HR department, frustration grew as they observed the lack of buy-in from line managers. And since managers lacked a broader understanding of the initiative, they saw age management as "just another" HR program that would not create value. Meanwhile, the 50+ workers whose hopes had been raised by new promises were disappointed in the end because they felt undervalued and no longer needed by their employer.

Age Management Problem #6: The Early Exit

Increased energy costs and high personnel expenses forced ChemCo, a publicly listed chemical company employing 6,500 people, to start a comprehensive cost-saving initiative. The company called for an extra board meeting during which the following conversation transpired:

Harry, ChemCo's CFO, advocated an early retirement solution: "We have done this at ChemCo in the past, and it's the fastest way to replace expensive (older) staff with younger, lower-cost people. It makes for a good story that will boost our weakening share price quite a bit."

There were nods around the room until Beth, the HR director, chimed in: "We do have an aging problem, as 38 percent of our staff is 50 years and older, but didn't we agree after our last workforce reduction not to use early retirement anymore? We all agreed that too many of our best leaders walked out the door, taking all their expertise along with them. Their institutional knowledge is incredible, and many older workers have been instrumental in nurturing the potential of our younger workforce. Isn't there another way of cutting costs?"

At this point, Tony, the CEO, who is known for a balanced view and longer-term perspective, added: "It'll hit our balance sheet hard in the short term. We're looking at increased pension liabilities and one-time costs for incentives. In the long run, we could see significant salary savings and a chance to restructure without layoffs. You all know we need to be more agile and productive, and our younger talent bench is hungry."

When John, the risk-aversive EVP of Controlling joined the conversation, he pointed to the ramifications that yet another early retirement plan would have on the culture and the trust people have in the loyalty of the firm to its workers: "I'm concerned about losing experienced talent. Can we ensure knowledge transfer?"

Beth replied, with a reminder that the company's knowledge transfer and mentoring programs did not really work last time. "People in phased retirement plans were not as committed as we thought they would be." Then she turned to the CEO and said, "Tony, the bigger question is: When are we actually going to take the demographic change seriously? We clearly need proactive foresight here. If we agree today to launch another early retirement program, we'll be telling our 50-58 cohort that we value and need you today, but the best we can do for you at ChemCo is early retirement in a few years."

Early retirement incentive programs have been a common downsizing strategy in modern times. They are seen as a way to reduce workforce expenses and address social issues like unemployment rates among younger workers. However, many governments have started abolishing state-financed early retirement pathways and are now aiming to extend working lives by postponing retirement ages.[27] Organizations are increasingly adopting more comprehensive age management strategies beyond just early retirement.[28]

For example, a study of Dutch organizations found that only 20.8 percent were classified as using early retirees mainly for standard work.[29] This suggests early retirement is not the dominant approach for most organizations.

There is growing recognition that early retirement should not be used as a "quick solution" and can have negative implications.[30] Organizations are now more likely to implement a range of age-related HR practices and policies aimed at retaining and supporting older workers, rather than encouraging early exits.[31]

Even so, despite positive efforts to tap into the potential of an aging workforce, in 2024 we saw several high-profile early retirement offer-

27 https://academic.oup.com/workar/article/7/4/257/6406531?login=false
28 https://www.cedefop.europa.eu/files/5544_en.pdf
29 https://academic.oup.com/gerontologist/article-abstract/55/3/374/587138?redirected-From=fulltext
30 https://www.emerald.com/insight/content/doi/10.1108/REPS-06-2019-0087/full/html
31 https://academic.oup.com/workar/article/7/4/257/6406531?login=false and https://www.cedefop.europa.eu/files/5544_en.pdf

ings as a means of downsizing, including the US Postal Service, SAP, Nissan, Volkswagen, and ThyssenKrupp.[32]

Age Management Problem #7: Allowing Negative Attitudes to Persist

Negative stereotypes and attitudes about aging will hinder your Wise Management initiatives. If allowed to persist, harmful perceptions will have wide-ranging impacts, not only on older adults' wellbeing, performance, and opportunities, but also on the success of age management initiatives.

Organizations may fail to leverage the skills, experience, and wisdom of older workers due to misperceptions about their abilities. Negative stereotypes can fuel conflict between younger and older workers, hindering collaboration and knowledge transfer—something that the organization must consider as part of its age management. Older workers who perceive age discrimination tend to have lower job satisfaction and work engagement,[33] so it should not surprise anyone when discriminated individuals choose not buy into the age management initiatives. Furthermore, ageist work environments push older workers toward early retirement, leading to a loss of valuable human capital.

When managers hold negative attitudes and stereotypes toward older employees, they undermine the effectiveness of age management initiatives. Several empirical studies have highlighted this issue: Research shows that negative stereotypes affect employers' hiring intentions and decisions regarding older workers.[34] This makes it more dif-

32 https://federalnewsnetwork.com/workforce/2025/01/usps-offers-up-to-15k-in-early-retirement-buyouts-to-cut-mail-handler-staffing/, https://www.reuters.com/business/autos-transportation/nissan-says-about-1000-us-staff-accept-early-retirement-2024-11-21/, https://group.mercedes-benz.com/dokumente/unternehmen/sonstiges/mercedes-benz-group-gbr-taetigkeitsbericht-2024.pdf, and https://www.heise.de/en/news/Severance-pay-retirement-Twice-as-many-employees-want-to-leave-SAP-as-planned-9753248.html

33 https://pmc.ncbi.nlm.nih.gov/articles/PMC9266066/

34 https://link.springer.com/article/10.1007/s10433-022-00720-3 and https://pmc.ncbi.nlm.nih.gov/articles/PMC8070998/

ficult for older employees to change jobs or re-enter the labor market if they lose their current position.

One study found that employees who perceived their managers to hold negative attitudes toward older workers had an increased risk of losing paid work within a two-year follow-up period.[35] The perception that "older workers create conflicts" was significantly associated with an increased risk of job loss. Two other negative attitudes—"older workers' qualifications are outdated" and "older workers cannot keep up with the pace and development"—were also linked to higher risk of losing paid work.

Contrary to the concept of a Wise Organization, negative stereotypes can become internalized by older workers, leading to reduced self-efficacy, uncertainty about their own performance, and greater likelihood of giving up work when facing challenges.

This can create a self-fulfilling prophecy, potentially impacting actual job performance and jeopardizing any activities to leverage the potential of their tenured workforce. Multiple studies have found associations between experiencing ageism and the desire or intention to retire early. One prospective analysis showed that perceived age discrimination was linked to early retirement intentions.

Age & the Annual Review

With the end of the fiscal year approaching, it was time again for the annual performance review, so Martha called for a meeting with Josh, her loyal 58-year-old VP of finance. The meeting started routinely going through the performance appraisal form. First, they reviewed Josh's goal achievements, then they discussed his major accomplishments. Next, they evaluated key competencies and arrived at an overall performance rating with areas of improvement noted.

When the discussion shifted to future goals and objectives, Martha made an off-hand comment: "Josh, at some point, we need to talk

---

35   https://link.springer.com/article/10.1007/s10433-022-00720-3

110

about your future. I mean, the firm needs to know when you want to leave." Josh thought about the job he liked so much and the favorable review he'd just received for the past year. Leaving was not on his radar. Trying to maintain a professional tone, Josh replied:

"I'd be open to discussing options at some point, perhaps a gradual transition or mentoring role if that would be helpful." To which, Martha said, "That's a constructive approach. We'll definitely explore those options. Now, switching gears slightly, is there anything the company can do to support you better, considering that you probably have some changing needs as you're getting older?"

Josh: "Well, I appreciate your asking. Some flexibility in working hours or the option to work from home occasionally would be helpful, especially on days when I have medical appointments."

Martha: "Thank you for sharing that. We'll certainly look into accommodating those needs. Is there anything else you'd like to discuss regarding your performance or future with the company?"

Josh: "Not at the moment, but I appreciate that you've initiated this conversation."

While Martha felt she'd "covered it all," Josh went back to his desk with the odd feeling that his relevance in the organization was rapidly diminishing and his professional standing in the firm was growing uncertain.

Age Management Problem #8: The Annual Performance Review

One of the most detrimental ways that organizations handle age management is by reducing it to the annual performance review conversation between a manager and an employee. Giving the employee an opportunity once a year to "ask for what you need" does not constitute an age management strategy. In fact, there are many problems with this approach.

First, a performance review is not the place to reflect upon one's purpose and future work contribution in the context of aging. Talking about age-related concerns and challenges is a sensitive, private topic that may not be easy to share with one's manager in full transparency. Second, an isolated conversation may lead to an outcome that would require a deeper understanding and better support structure for the intended action to be fruitful. And third, the respective manager may not have sufficient knowledge of the subject matter and could be influenced by personal bias.

> Nick returned from a workshop with fellow 50+ workers during which they had gathered to talk about new and different ways to leverage professional experience. Organized by the company's HR department as part of an age management initiative, the workshop made Nick feel proud of his experience and empowered to leverage it in a more effective way.
>
> One day, he presented an idea to his boss, Tony, for improving the productivity of the 50+ cohort. Nick went on to explain that he felt stuck in a silo and that the lack of cross-sectoral activity prevented him—and probably others—from leveraging his knowledge and experience more effectively.
>
> Instead of welcoming the input, Tony responded by emphasizing the risks involved in changing the existing work patterns, and he failed to acknowledge the potential upside. Over the next few weeks, Nick circled back several times, unfortunately without success, leaving him to wonder why he had attended the workshop in the first place.

Three additional factors can prevent age management initiatives from succeeding:

Lack of organizational support: The absence of proper organizational support can severely hamper age-related management initiatives. Without backing from senior management, strategic Wise Management efforts are unlikely to succeed.[36] Moreover, an unsupportive HR environment and lack of sufficient budget block the implementation of best practices. Failure to secure commitment from aging workers themselves may also lead to resistance for Wise Management programs.

Poor manager involvement: Anyone who manages people in an organization needs to understand the bigger picture and acquire specific knowledge about the nature of aging in work environments. Many leaders believe that additional training and involvement are not necessary, as they feel sufficiently equipped. Even worse, they may worry that admitting their lack of expertise in this field would be seen as a weakness, so they avoid getting involved.

Another sign of poor age management practices happens when engaged older workers seek ways to leverage their experience in different ways, and their managers show little interest in reinterpreting roles. It may be more convenient for the manager to keep work patterns unchanged, but the company loses an opportunity to benefit from its experienced talent base.

Ignoring differences among older people: Treating older workers as a homogeneous group, rather than acknowledging variations in job types, physical and cognitive requirements, and the role of experience invariably leads to failed age management efforts.[37]

Contrary to the examples outlined above, effective Wise Management requires a holistic, fully supported strategy that combats stereotypes, engages older workers, and recognizes the diverse needs and potential contributions of an aging workforce.

---

36 https://edz.bib.uni-mannheim.de/www-edz/pdf/ef/98/ef9865en.pdf
37 https://pmc.ncbi.nlm.nih.gov/articles/PMC7681210/

CHAPTER 5 SUMMARY

Once an organization has committed to addressing the challenges of the demographic shift and provide specific solutions, it is paramount to consider the interdependencies of the various initiatives, and to be aware of the "ticking the box" phenomenon: "We address the needs of our older workers by offering more job flexibility and more development opportunities." The same applies to a common belief that the challenge of an aging workforce can be solved by simply adding the topic to the DEI agenda. And, last but not least, investing time in assuring the appropriate level of organizational support will go a long way toward realizing success.

Chapter 6
HR's Silver Lining: Shifting from Human Resources to People and Culture

Have you noticed that many companies are changing the name of their personnel function from Human Resources to People and Culture? This renaming mirrors a fundamental shift in how organizations value employees and shape the corporate culture. It is also indicative of places that are more likely to prioritize age diversity and intergenerational collaboration.

The shift from "Human Resources" (HR) to "People and Culture" (P&C) reflects a significant evolution in how organizations approach workforce management. Companies that make this change are usually trying to create a more holistic, employee-centered environment that emphasizes engagement, wellbeing, and alignment with organizational values. It's a perspective that has a huge impact on how companies manage intergenerational relationships within the workforce.

Why is this shift happening now? Let's explore the top four reasons:

1. **Holistic approach:** P&C signifies a broader focus beyond traditional HR functions, which focus on administrative tasks, such as payroll and compliance. P&C aims to foster a positive workplace culture that supports employee engagement and aligns with the organization's mission.[38]

2. **Employee experience:** Organizations increasingly recognize that a positive employee experience is crucial for attracting and retaining talent. The P&C approach emphasizes creating environments

---

38   https://www.aihr.com/blog/people-and-culture/ and https://www.linkedin.com/pulse/human-resources-vs-people-culture-boney-eyamin-plabon/

where employees feel valued and empowered, which can lead to higher productivity and satisfaction.[39]

3. **Strategic alignment:** The transition to P&C is also about integrating people strategies with overall business goals. This perspective positions P&C as a vital component of organizational success, rather than limiting it to a support function.[40]

4. **Cultural relevance:** The term "Human Resources" has been criticized for treating employees as mere resources or commodities. By contrast, People and Culture reflects a commitment to valuing individuals and their contributions in meaningful ways that foster a sense of belonging and community within the workplace.[41]

Key differences between HR and P&C:

Aspect	Human Resources	People and Culture
Focus	Administrative tasks	Employee engagement and culture
Role	Support function	Strategic partner
Goals	Compliance and process management	Long-term organizational success
Employee perspective	Viewed as resources	Valued individuals

As you can see in the table above, the transition from Human Resources to People and Culture represents more than just a change in terminology; it signifies a fundamental shift in how organizations view their workforces. By adopting this new framework, companies aim to create environments that nurture talent, promote inclusivity, and align

39 https://www.fitzgeraldhr.co.uk/people-and-culture-human-resources/
40 https://www.forbes.com/councils/forbeshumanresourcescouncil/2023/02/08/why-and-how-to-evolve-from-human-resources-to-people-and-culture/
41 https://www.fitzgeraldhr.co.uk/people-and-culture-human-resources/

employee experiences with broader business objectives. I believe this evolution is essential in today's competitive landscape, where employee satisfaction directly influences organizational performance.

By cultivating a positive organizational culture, P&C departments become well-positioned to implement strategies that promote diversity and intergenerational collaboration. This focus helps companies retain older workers because they feel a sense of belonging and respect.[42]

Positive Drivers Toward Wise Management

In the context of this developing trend from HR to P&C, how do companies come to realize they need to do something about the aging workforce? In my observations, awareness tends to develop somewhat randomly, often from a combination of internal and external factors. It may start with HR managers noticing shifts in the workforce composition. They begin to see a larger proportion of their employees approaching retirement age. As explained in Chapter 1, this trend is particularly pronounced in regions with low birth rates and increasing life expectancy.[43]

As the EVP HR of a leading testing, inspection, and certification (TIC) company put it: "If you want to create awareness for this challenge, it brings to mind the expression, 'How to eat an elephant? In pieces!' At TIC, we are used to looking at numbers and being precise. Hence, we ran the HR data analytics detailing the number of individuals retiring in the near future and what skills need to be replaced in what timeframe. This frames the problem in our language and creates awareness. And to assure that our employer brand is strong enough, we gathered data around hiring expectations of younger talent (pre- and post-hiring) and made adjustments for better alignment."

---

42   https://www.elsevier.es/en-revista-tekhne-review-applied-management-350-articulo-man-aging-an-aging-workforce-what-S1645991115000080 and http://www.ageingatwork.eu/resources/a-guide-to-good-practice-in-age-management.pdf

43   https://www.wifor.com/en/demographic-change/

As older workers retire, recruiters in the organization may struggle to find younger employees with the necessary skills and experience to replace them. This creates a noticeable skills gap within the company.[44] Next, people managers may find that traditional incentive systems, such as the usual upward career opportunities, fail to motivate older employees.

Increased conflicts sometimes develop when managers engage with the senior segment of their workforce. ("They aren't adapting the way we need them to adapt.") And HR notices a growing concern in the organization about losing valuable institutional knowledge and expertise as experienced employees retire.

Beside these internal drivers, HR may also face external pressures that highlight the need for action. As the labor market tightens and the working-age population shrinks, companies will experience increased difficulty in recruiting and retaining talent.[45] Shifts in the age structure of the population can alter market demands, requiring organizations to adapt their products or services. Finally, governments may introduce new policies or regulations to address demographic challenges, compelling organizations to comply and adapt.[46]

From Awareness to Commitment

Even once leaders acknowledge the imperative to develop a Wise Management strategy, how do they get from recognition to committed action?

Patrick, the P&C director at FoodCorp, sat in his office, poring over employee data. As he scrolled through the charts, a stark reality hit him: The company's workforce was aging rapidly, with a significant portion

---

44 https://great2know.de/en/blog/successfully-tackling-demographic-change-in-germa-ny-as-a-company/

45 https://reform-support.ec.europa.eu/our-projects/flagship-technical-support-projects/tsi-2025-flagship-tackling-demographic-change-through-supporting-skills-labour-market-and-social_en

46 https://reform-support.ec.europa.eu/our-projects/flagship-technical-support-projects/tsi-2025-flagship-tackling-demographic-change-through-supporting-skills-labour-market-and-social_en

nearing retirement age. Patrick was aware of the demographic change in general, but he didn't fully appreciate its consequences. His heart raced as he contemplated the implications. Skills gaps, loss of institutional knowledge, and a shrinking talent pool loomed on the horizon. Patrick knew that if left unchecked, this demographic shift could severely impact the company's future. "But will I even still be here as this trend takes hold, or is it going to happen much farther out in the future?" he wondered.

That evening, Patrick couldn't sleep. He tossed and turned, his mind filled with potential consequences, but more importantly missed opportunities. As dawn broke, so did his resolve. He realized that mere awareness wasn't enough; action was imperative. He thought, "I owe it to myself—I need to capitalize on these opportunities for the benefit of my career and FoodCorp."

Within the P&C function of any given organization, there isn't typically an age management "department." In Chapter 5, we looked at the negative consequences of having fuzzy accountability for this problem, but we haven't identified who should be responsible.

In our work at WiseForce Advisors, we frequently see an unstructured and opportunistic approach to solving these problems. In some cases, the effort comes from an individual who sees this as an opportunity to shine and shape their career. In other cases, an older P&C professional, who is experiencing ageism, decides to elevate the issue. It's especially helpful when a CHRO who is close to retirement and understands the implications of an aging workforce firsthand leads the charge. Another path is for the most senior P&C leader to put the age management topic on the department's strategy agenda, demonstrating a bigger understanding of the long-term, strategic implications.

However the topic makes its way to the P&C agenda, decision-makers on the receiving end often lack sufficient knowledge of age management strategies and best practices. They need to recognize who or what is driving the age agenda. Is it the Diversity & Inclusion function that frames age management as a diversity issue? Or a younger professional who sees the problem as one of intergenerational communication? Or is it a marketer who wants to adopt a positive-sounding label for older workers, such as Wise Peers (Altana AG) or Wisdom Workers (Allianz SE)?

From Commitment to Strategy

Marion, the Chief People Officer of the market-leading building materials company FineBuild Corp, opened her laptop to review the results gained from a diagnostic workshop her team had done to assess their readiness for building a Wise Organization. One key insight from the workshop was that the firm's two core pillars for the mid-term strategy, "transform and perform," would be influenced by the demographic change.

Scrolling through the slide deck, Marion paused at the guiding principles of FineBuild's age diversity initiative. These principles serve as a framework to counter the challenges and are understood to foster initiatives for future change and prosperity. Marion felt happy, as she realized that the diagnostic workshop not only confirmed the company's commitment but also inspired so many ideas for their strategy and corresponding actions to take.

Marion closed her computer thinking, "As a next step, let's make a detailed strategic plan, define processes, create role models, and support it with targeted communication." Then she called her boss, and committed to presenting a strategy at the next board meeting.

Several factors will shape how the age agenda plays out in an organization. It depends on the way P&C is organized, whether P&C is embedded in other functions as a partner to the business, and the overall image of P&C in the organization (as a business driver with a high level of involvement or a function that provides resources upon request), and finally, the underlying corporate culture.

Here are some examples of how the age agenda can take shape:

1. **Strategic Planning and Risk Assessment:** As these challenges become more apparent, organizations typically respond through workforce planning in which P&C conducts analyses to forecast future workforce needs and identify potential gaps; risk manage-

ment when P&C and the business assess the potential impact of demographic change on its operations, productivity, and competitiveness; and strategic reviews during which leadership teams incorporate demographic trends into their long-term strategic planning processes.

2. **Competitive Pressure:** P&C may be spurred to action by observing competitors and noticing other firms in the industry implementing strategies to address demographic challenges.[47] As the pool of available workers shrinks, organizations face increased competition for skilled employees, and in this way competition for talent can become a strong motivator for change.[48]

3. **Proactive Measures:** Forward-thinking organizations take preemptive action. They may invest in data collection and analysis to understand demographic trends affecting their workforce and market. Some organizations will launch programs to foster innovation and knowledge transfer among generations.[49]

By recognizing these three signs, organizations can begin to develop and implement strategies to address the challenges posed by demographic change, ensuring their long-term sustainability and competitiveness.

As a further consideration, P&C should implement evidence-based age management practices that have been shown to be effective, such as flexibility practices to enhance engagement and performance, maintenance P&C practices for older workers (e.g., tenure anniversaries or health maintenance support), and development opportunities tailored to different age groups.[50]

---

47 https://great2know.de/en/blog/successfully-tackling-demographic-change-in-germany-as-a-company/

48 https://reform-support.ec.europa.eu/our-projects/flagship-technical-support-projects/tsi-2025-flagship-tackling-demographic-change-through-supporting-skills-labour-market-and-social_en

49 https://great2know.de/en/blog/successfully-tackling-demographic-change-in-germany-as-a-company/

50 https://academic.oup.com/workar/article/7/4/257/6406531?login=false

Manager Engagement

Line managers play a crucial role in implementing Wise Management practices. P&C should provide training to managers, making sure that all leaders understand the importance of the topic, how behavioral change unfolds as people age, and how it impacts performance, the pitfalls of unconscious bias, and how to turn an aging workforce into a competitive advantage.

No matter how an organization arrives at the conclusion that it's time to get serious about age management, strategic alignment is paramount for success. P&C must align its initiatives with overall organizational goals and strategies.

As you are shaping your organization as a Wise Organization, start with aligning your Wise Management strategy with your corporate vision and objectives. Wise Organizations use the following framework:

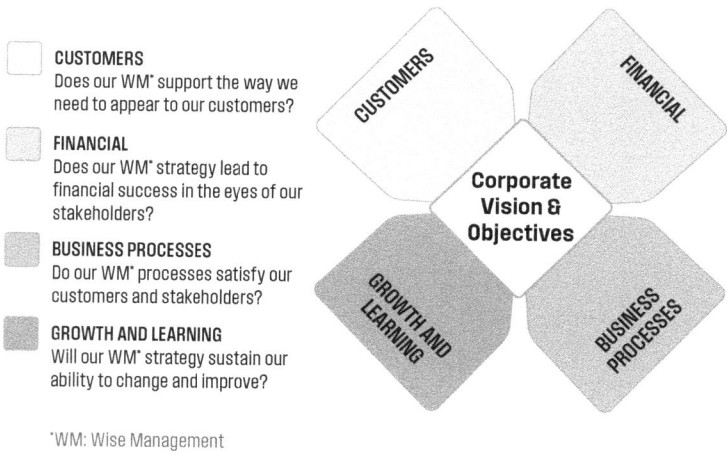

CUSTOMERS
Does our WM* support the way we need to appear to our customers?

FINANCIAL
Does our WM* strategy lead to financial success in the eyes of our stakeholders?

BUSINESS PROCESSES
Do our WM* processes satisfy our customers and stakeholders?

GROWTH AND LEARNING
Will our WM* strategy sustain our ability to change and improve?

*WM: Wise Management

Wise Organizations follow a simple three-step-process:
1. Revisit your corporate vision and objectives.
2. Brainstorm how an aging and age-diverse workforce could contribute to achieving those goals.

3. Evaluate how the potential age management initiatives that you've considered so far would align with the company's mission and values. Then answer the questions in the framework to assess whether your potential age management initiatives are sufficient and fully aligned with your corporate objectives. As you answer these questions and assign your first age management initiatives to one of the four dimensions, a first cut of your Wise Management strategy takes shape. Additional iterations will help to refine this strategy.

As a next step, you're going to integrate this new Wise Management strategy into your overall People and Culture strategy:
1. Review existing HR policies and practices.
2. Identify areas where the various elements of your Wise Management strategy can be incorporated into the wider P&C strategy.
3. Ensure consistency with other intergenerational and/or DEI initiatives.

The Importance of Scalability

In my experience, it is difficult to move an organization from perceiving the demographic challenge as an important concern to designating it an urgent problem to solve. Even so, it is critical to understand that the scalability of any early Wise Management initiative has a decisive effect on the organization's ability to build and maintain momentum.

Allianz Group, a leading insurance company, provides a great example of this truism. Its Wisdom Workers are seasoned professionals who participate in the company's New Joiner Mentoring Program.[51] Through this initiative, experienced workers pair up with new employees to share their knowledge and expertise. The program is designed to facilitate knowledge transfer and support the integration of new employees into the company culture.

---

51 https://www.linkedin.com/posts/allianz_diversity-agediversity-agediversityday-activity-7243980189012004866-H3sL/

Allianz currently hires about 20,000 people per year, and through this mentoring program, the company creates 20,000 meaningful touchpoints and new connections annually. It fosters intergenerational learning, cultural transmission, and visibility of experience, which creates a multiplier effect.

The mentoring program aligns with Allianz's focus on learning and development, which is a key part of its employee satisfaction strategy.[52] By leveraging the experience of its highly valued Wisdom Workers, Allianz aims to create a culture of continuous learning, and support growth and development across the entire workforce.

Building Your Wise Organization

As a first step toward building your Wise Organization, review the current vs. optimal states in each of the following areas:

Policy

- Review current policies for recruitment, retention, and retirement in light of an aging workforce.
- Evaluate flexible work arrangements to accommodate different life stages.
- Evaluate current mentoring and knowledge transfer programs.

Training and Development

- To what extent are the learning and development opportunities age-neutral?
- Review training offers for age bias and intergenerational collaboration.
- Evaluate career planning support for all age groups.

Work Environment

- Evaluate the workplace design for ergonomic qualities and accessibility.
- Review health and wellbeing initiatives for all ages.
- How inclusive is the culture? Does it value diverse perspectives?

---

52 https://www.allianz-trade.com/en_global/news-insights/expert-voices/investing-in-people.html

Performance Management

- How fair and unbiased are the performance evaluation systems?
- To what extent are performance expectations age-neutral?
- How are contributions recognized and rewarded, regardless of age?

Succession Planning

- Evaluate the talent pipelines across all age groups.
- Evaluate phased retirement options.
- Review knowledge retention strategies.

Communication and Engagement

- Evaluate the encouragement of intergenerational collaboration and knowledge sharing.
- How effective and insightful is the gathering of regular feedback from employees of all ages?
- Evaluate the promotion of age diversity benefits to all stakeholders.

Mistakes that P&C Needs to Avoid

It's easy for P&C professionals to make mistakes when starting to create a Wise Organization. Here are some of the biggest pitfalls to avoid:

Failing to Take a Holistic Approach

Wise Management requires a comprehensive strategy that spans the entire employee lifecycle. Implementing isolated or piecemeal initiatives without considering how they fit into the broader organizational context will invariably cause problems down the road. Effective Wise Management addresses recruitment, training, career development, health and safety, flexible work arrangements, and retirement transitions in an integrated manner.

Lack of Top-Level Commitment

Implementing Wise Management practices without securing genuine commitment from top management is a recipe for failure. HR needs to ensure that there is leadership buy-in and a clear strategy for your Wise Management initiative.[53] Without the support of senior leadership, HR may struggle to implement meaningful organizational change.

Relying on Stereotypes and Biases

One of the most critical mistakes happens when decision-makers base their age management practices on stereotypes and biases about different age groups. This can lead to discriminatory practices and reinforce negative perceptions.[54] HR should avoid making assumptions about employees' capabilities, interests, or needs based solely on their age.

Inadequate Communication

Poor communication about transformation initiatives can lead to misunderstandings and resistance. P&C should clearly articulate the benefits of age diversity and management practices to all employees, regardless of their age. I strongly advise collaborating with communication experts for this step.

Insufficient Age-Specific Practices

Despite recognizing the importance of age management, many organizations still lack comprehensive age-related HR practices. This gap between awareness and implementation can hinder efforts to effectively manage the aging workforce.[55]

53 http://www.ageingatwork.eu/resources/taen-guide-to-age-management-sept-07.pdf
54 https://www.shrm.org/topics-tools/news/five-tips-avoiding-age-discrimination and https://www.inclusiveemployers.co.uk/blog/how-to-manage-age-diversity-in-the-workplace/
55 https://www.redalyc.org/journal/5538/553863219002/html/

Inadequate Manager Training

Line managers play a key role in implementing Wise Management practices. Insufficient age diversity training can undermine P&C's efforts.

Failing to Keep Momentum

Typically, once P&C has started a Wise Management transformation initiative, stakeholders at all levels recognize this as a new and promising agenda. Intrinsically, everyone knows about the impact that the aging demographic is having on the organization and recognizes that actions have to be taken. It's important to use that initial excitement and stoke the fire to keep the momentum going. If organizations fail to keep the drumbeat going, existing stereotypes and attitudes will resurface, creating a barrier for successful implementation.

Lack of Follow-Through

P&C may have launched its first initiative to address the aging workforce, raising awareness of the topic and creating an expectation in the workforce that things will change. But a lack of follow-through after the announcement will lead to disappointment and resentment, which could do more harm than good.

By being aware of these dynamics and potential pitfalls, HR professionals can drive the Wise Management agenda within their organizations. I hope I've convinced you that success requires a strategic, holistic approach that goes beyond surface-level initiatives to embed an age-inclusive mindset and practices throughout every level of the organization.

CHAPTER 6 SUMMARY

The People and Culture function is a key player in crafting a Wise Management agenda that is linked to the corporate strategy and backed by key stakeholders. As P&C rolls out the new strategy, it needs to realign age-related practices, eliminate age stereotypes, provide adequate manager training, and harness the organizational dynamics to keep the momentum going strong.

Chapter 7
Beyond the Young and Restless: Leveling Up Your Diversity Game

To understand how Wise Management aligns with diversity and inclusion (D&I), we need to revisit the history of this movement. The concept of D&I has its roots in the civil rights movement of the 1950s and 1960s in the United States. However, its evolution into the modern understanding of D&I in the workplace has been a gradual process, spanning several decades.

The Early Foundations (1950s–1960s) saw significant legal milestones that addressed discrimination. (The Civil Rights Act of 1964 prohibited discrimination based on race, color, religion, sex, or national origin.)[56] At this stage, the focus was primarily on eliminating overt discrimination and ensuring basic civil rights, rather than embracing diversity as we understand it today.

This period was followed by the Affirmative Action Era (1970s–1980s), when organizations began implementing programs to increase representation of underrepresented groups.[57] The focus was mainly on compliance with legal requirements and increasing demographic diversity.

In the early 1980s, the concept of diversity training began to take shape: Lewis Brown Griggs, the US Executive Leadership Coach and Facilitator, coined the terms "diversity" and "equity" in the workplace context.[58] In the 1980s, companies started implementing diverse training programs to help employees adjust to changing work environments.

---

56 https://oxford-review.com/what-is-dei-the-oxford-review-guide-to-diversity-equity-and-inclusion/ and https://diversityofficermagazine.com/diversity-inclusion/the-history-of-diversity-training-its-pioneers/
57 https://www.inclusiongeeks.com/articles/a-history-of-dei-and-the-future-of-work/
58 https://guidetohr.com/the-origin-of-dei/

The 1990s and 2000s saw a shift toward embracing multiculturalism. The focus expanded beyond race and gender to include a broader range of identities and backgrounds. Organizations began to recognize the value of diverse perspectives in the workplace. Around 2000, the concept evolved into what we now know as Diversity, Equity, and Inclusion (DEI).

In 2009, Lester A. Lefton at Kent University formed the University Diversity Action Council, marking a more formal approach to DEI in higher education. There is now an increased emphasis in organizations on creating inclusive environments where all individuals feel respected and valued. The scope has expanded to include various dimensions of diversity, such as sexual orientation, disability, age, and more.

DEI Leads to Better Business Outcomes

In December 2023, McKinsey & Company published its fourth report on Diversity and Inclusion titled: "Diversity matters even more: The case for holistic impact."[59] In this report, McKinsey delivered a comprehensive global perspective on the relationship between leadership diversity and company performance. For 2023, the business case was the strongest it had been since the firm began tracking these metrics and, for the first time in some areas, equitable representation is in sight.

Furthermore, a striking new finding is that leadership diversity is also convincingly associated with holistic growth ambitions, greater social impact, and more satisfied workforces. The data showed a clear correlation between diversity and performance that has been progressing over time.

McKinsey's 2015 report found top-quartile companies (those embracing DEI) had a 15 percent greater likelihood of financial outperformance versus their bottom-quartile peers; in 2023, that figure hit 39 percent:

---

59   https://www.mckinsey.com/featured-insights/diversity-and-inclusion/diversity-matters-even-more-the-case-for-holistic-impact

The business case for diversity on executive teams and financial outperformance

Difference in likelihood of outperformance of 1st vs. 4th quartile[1]

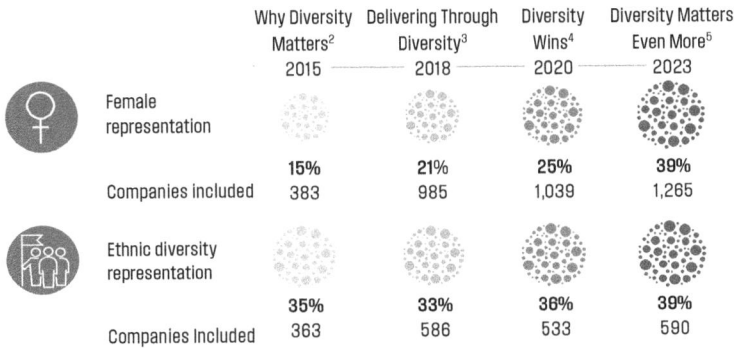

		Why Diversity Matters[2] 2015	Delivering Through Diversity[3] 2018	Diversity Wins[4] 2020	Diversity Matters Even More[5] 2023
	Female representation				
		15%	21%	25%	39%
	Companies included	383	985	1,039	1,265
	Ethnic diversity representation				
		35%	33%	36%	39%
	Companies Included	363	586	533	590

In 2023, eight new countries were incorporated into gender analyses and two new countries for ethnicity analyses

1   Likelihood of financial outperformance vs. the regional industry median. p-value for regression analysis < 0.01.
2   Gender: n = 383; ethnicity: n = 363; US, UK, and Latin America. Average EBIT margin 2010-13.
3   Gender: n = 985; Australia, Brazil, France, Germany, India, Japan, Mexico, Nigeria, Singapore, South Africa, UK, and US; ethnicity: n = 586; Brazil, Mexico, Singapore, South Africa, UK and US; average EBIT margin 2011-15.
4   Gender: n = 1,039; 2017 companies for which gender data was available in 2019 plus Denmark, Norway, and Sweden; ethnicity: n = 533; 2017 companies for which ethnicity data was available in 2019; average EBIT margin 2014-18.
5   Gender: n = 1,265; 2019 companies for which gender data was available in 2022 plus Canada, Colombia, Egypt, Israel, Italy, Malaysia, New Zealand, and Spain; ethnicity: n =590 ;19 companies for which ethnicity data was available in 2022 plus Canada and New Zealand; average EBIT margin 2017-21.

The last decade has been a period of notable progress on equitable representation in leadership. Yet representation is an insufficient and unsustainable outcome. Since publishing its report "Why Diversity Matters" in 2015, McKinsey's thinking has evolved with continued engagement in this field. From their initial focus on diverse representation in leadership, the authors added a perspective on the practical steps companies can take to increase leadership diversity. From there, they broadened the focus to highlight the value of inclusion and equity.

Currently, organizations focus their diversity and inclusion initiatives around the following areas, differing in commitment, intensity, cohesion, and follow-through (e.g., their DEI focus centers on representation, but not on culture; or focusing on inclusive leadership training, but not linking DEI actively to productivity improvement initiatives):

Representation and Leadership

Organizations are placing significant emphasis on increasing diversity at all levels, particularly in leadership positions;[60] setting specific targets for representation, such as achieving gender parity or increasing racial/ethnic diversity in executive teams;[61] and implementing policies to ensure fair treatment in hiring, pay, and promotions.[62]

Inclusive Culture

We are seeing a growing recognition that diversity alone is not enough, and companies are focusing on creating an environment where all employees feel valued, respected, and supported,[63] promoting openness and tackling microaggressions, bias, and discrimination; fostering a sense of belonging for all employees.

Measurement and Accountability

Some organizations put more emphasis on linking D&I efforts to business performance, innovation, and productivity—and recognizing D&I as not just an ethical imperative but a strategic business necessity.

60 https://sustainabilitymag.com/top10/top-10-diverse-leadership-teams and https://www.socialtalent.com/blog/diversity-and-inclusion/9-companies-around-the-world-that-are-embracing-diversity

61 https://www.mckinsey.com/featured-insights/mckinsey-explainers/what-is-diversity-equity-and-inclusion

62 https://www.ilo.org/resource/news/greater-progress-diversity-and-inclusion-essential-rebuild-productive-and

63 https://www.nucamp.co/blog/coding-bootcamp-full-stack-web-and-mobile-development-how-can-tech-companies-measure-the-success-of-their-diversity-initiatives

Employee Engagement and Development

Still other organizations are prioritizing Employee Resource Groups (ERGs) to support diverse communities and their allies,[64] and inclusive leadership training and development programs, as well as mentorship and sponsorship programs to support career advancement for underrepresented groups.

Transparency and Reporting

Establishing clear objectives and metrics to track progress on D&I initiatives involves steps such as implementing comprehensive diversity reports and dashboards, and tying executive compensation to diversity goals to ensure accountability.

Broader Definition of Diversity

The concept of diversity is expanding to include gender, race, ethnicity, age, disability status, neurodiversity, and LGBTQ+ identities. It is also important to recognize that individuals may belong to multiple underrepresented groups.

Business Impact

There's an increased emphasis on publishing diversity data and progress reports,[65] and on being transparent about pay equity and working toward closing any gaps.

Despite all of this progress, however, D&I is beginning to experience diminishing funding and management support, as described in this Forbes article.[66] The trend, known as "diversity fatigue," has several underlying causes, including:

---

64 https://www.socialtalent.com/blog/diversity-and-inclusion/9-compa-
    nies-around-the-world-that-are-embracing-diversity
65 https://www.mckinsey.com/featured-insights/mckinsey-explainers/what-is-diversity-equi-
    ty-and-inclusion
66 https://www.forbes.com/sites/shaunharper/2023/07/18/why-corporate-execs-are-pulling-
    the-plug-on-dei/

- **Shifting priorities:** D&I is often seen as important but not urgent, leading to deprioritization.[67]
- **Economic pressure:** Moreover, during times of economic downturn or crisis, companies view D&I as a "luxury we cannot afford."[68]
- **Perceived lack of progress:** One of the primary reasons for D&I fatigue is the perception that these efforts are not yielding tangible results.[69] When D&I initiatives seem slow-moving or lack visible outcomes, it can lead to discouragement and a sense of futility among those involved.
- **Oversaturation and burnout:** A continuous focus on diversity topics can become overwhelming, leading to information-overload and disengagement from the subject altogether.

While a noticeable diversity fatigue has been building quietly over time, the most recent developments after the 2024 US presidential election is remarkable:

1. **Political pressure:** The current political climate, including executive orders signed by President Trump to reverse DEI efforts in the federal workforce, has created pressure on companies to reduce or eliminate their DEI programs.[70]
2. **Public backlash:** Social media campaigns led by conservative influencers have targeted companies with DEI initiatives, leading to negative publicity.[71]
3. **Legal challenges:** The US Supreme Court's ruling against affirmative action in college admissions has emboldened conservative activists to target workplace DEI programs through lawsuits.

67   https://quantive.com/resources/articles/dei-challenges
68   https://www.mckinsey.com/~/media/mckinsey/featured%20insights/diversity%20and%20 inclusion/diversity%20wins%20how%20inclusion%20matters/diversity-wins-how-inclusion-matters-vf.pdf
69   https://www.marchingsheep.com/diversity-fatigue-is-real-and-dangerous/
70   https://www.hrdive.com/news/companies-to-weaken-dei-commitments-in-2025/738219/ and https://www.cnn.com/2025/01/22/us/dei-diversity-equity-inclusion-explained/index.html
71   https://time.com/7209960/companies-rolling-back-dei/ and https://www.nbcnews.com/news/nbcblk/anti-dei-program-effort-2025-states-companies-universities-trump-rcna184580

In parallel, some companies are redirecting funds from DEI initiatives to general operating expenses, AI, or technology initiatives.[72] And about 40 percent of companies still view diversity primarily as an issue of compliance rather than a strategic business imperative.[73]

Age as an Element of Diversity

Despite the general importance of D&I and against the backdrop of the current diversity fatigue, it is worth noting that "age" has not become a key element of most DEI initiatives. According to a 2017 PWC Corporate Directors Survey,[74] 91 percent of directors stated that age diversity is either very important or somewhat important for diversity of thought in the boardroom. Contrast that response with the known facts that only 60 percent of companies globally have a diversity, equity and inclusion agenda, while only 8 percent include age in the initiative. By recognizing age as a crucial aspect of diversity, companies can harness the full potential of a multi-generational workforce and create a more inclusive environment for all employees.

Age Diversity at Innov.Tech

Sarah, a respected DEI leader at Innov.Tech, recognized the need to expand the company's diversity initiatives to include age as a consideration. She implemented a series of programs to address ageism and promote intergenerational collaboration.

First, Sarah revamped the company's training materials to include age-diverse examples and to challenge age stereotypes. She then launched a reverse mentoring program, pairing younger employees with senior staff to exchange skills and perspectives. To attract a wider talent pool, Sarah worked with HR to remove age-biased language from job postings and implement age-blind initial screenings.

---

72 https://www.hrdive.com/news/companies-to-weaken-dei-commitments-in-2025/738219/
73 https://www.customerengagementinsider.com/employee-experience/articles/exposed-big-brands-like-nike-amazon-abandoning-dei
74 https://www.pwc.nl/nl/actueel-publicaties/assets/pdfs/age-diversity.pdf

> *She also introduced flexible work arrangements to accommodate employees at different life stages.*
>
> *The results were remarkable. Innov.Tech saw a double digit increase in innovation output and a well above average percent boost in problem-solving efficiency. Employee engagement scores rose significantly, with older workers reporting feeling more valued and younger employees gaining confidence in their contributions.*
>
> *By fostering an age-inclusive environment, Innov.Tech reaped the benefits of diverse organizations: enhanced creativity, improved decision-making, and stronger business results. The company's success story became a case study in how age diversity can drive both inclusivity and business growth in the industry.*

Leaving Age Out of Diversity Fosters Ageism

Franciska Krings, a Professor of Organizational Behavior at HEC Lausanne, recently published "The Impact of Diversity Statements: More than Just Window Dressing?"[75] Her previous work, "Too Old to Be Included: Age Diversity Statements Foster Diversity Yet Fall Short on Inclusion," also covers this topic.

Her research shows consistent evidence that, when building teams, short diversity statements (signed by the CEO, short commitments to age-diversity) increase the selection rate of older individuals, so that teams are more age-balanced, independently of the decision-makers' own ages or attitudes toward age and older workers. However, even if short diversity statements effectively increase the representation of older people in teams, they only boost inclusion if the organization shows a true commitment to change.

Excluding older people is still one of the most accepted forms of workplace prejudice. Many younger employees don't even need to be ashamed of their attitudes—dismissing older peoples' skills and per-

---

75   https://wp.unil.ch/hecoutreach/age-diversity-statements-change-workplace-behaviour/

spectives as outdated or less relevant. Age is, therefore, one of the most neglected areas when it comes to DEI.

Age bias, or ageism, is a largely neglected component of the diversity, equity, and inclusion decision-making dynamic that impacts both younger and older workers—and their respective performance on the job.

By actively embracing the potential of different age perspectives at work (as part of a DEI strategy), the adage "Ageism is the only acceptable bias left" could finally become a statement of the past.

Toward Generational Synergy

I believe it's time for a new approach that includes age in DEI concepts and initiatives. Given the current diversity fatigue and the pressure on improved business performance, organizations should shift the attention from diversity of underrepresented groups (omitting age as an important element) to fostering a culture of belonging and leveraging intergenerational diversity as a driver of innovation and performance.

Companies need to recognize the demographic changes that are unfolding and bring age into DEI. There is great new potential to be unleashed that will generate positive business outcomes. The opportunity lies in the dynamic arising from different levels of experience, knowledge, and strengths.

The Wise Organization must include age in its DEI approach. Here are just some of the ways you'll benefit from focusing on generational synergy (and age-diverse teams):[76]

1. **Enhanced innovation and creativity:** Companies with mixed age ranges are 1.7 times more likely to be innovation leaders in their market. This is due to the unique blend of fresh ideas from younger employees and the wisdom and experience provided by older employees.

---

76   https://welovesalt.com/news/job-market-insights/multi-generational-teams-age-diversity/

2. **Better decision-making:** Age- and gender-diverse teams make better decisions 80 percent of the time. The combination of varied life experiences and viewpoints from different generations can spark creative solutions and lead to more balanced and effective decision-making.[77]

3. **Increased productivity:** Studies show that age-diverse teams perform significantly better, delivering improved business outcomes in close to 90 percent of cases. Both younger and older workers are more productive in an age-diverse environment than with peers of the same age.

4. **Improved problem-solving:** Teams representing different age groups have more intellectual capital and reduce negative age-related bias, increasing employee engagement and leading to better problem-solving outcomes.[78]

5. **Enhanced performance on complex tasks:** Research on US federal tax employees found that age diversity correlated positively with performance in groups solving complex decision-making tasks.[79] This effect was particularly strong when tasks required complex decision-making without high time pressure.

By leveraging these benefits, organizations can create more effective and high-performing teams as they intentionally bring together perspectives from every generation. Likewise, "upping" their diversity game by embracing the "generational synergy" will also reduce ageism. In this way, organizations could benefit from evidence-based diversity principles that include "age" as a category to represent and include. Imagine working in a place where age diversity is valued and achieved, leading to better business performance, within a culture that fosters belonging and purpose.

77 https://talentor.com/blog/enhancing-the-value-of-age-diversity-in-teams-why-wisdom-work-is-the-new-knowledge-work
78 https://greatergood.berkeley.edu/article/item/why_age_diversity_is_a_strength_at_work
79 https://gfa2016.gesellschaft-fuer-arbeitswissenschaft.de/inhalt/C.6.11.pdf

CHAPTER 7 SUMMARY

Despite significant efforts and encouraging research that shows the positive impact DEI has on organizations, companies still seem to struggle to leverage the true power of diversity initiatives. One of the reasons may be that DEI is not sufficiently linked to business purpose and objectives. Including "age" as a category within the organization's DEI focus is highly recommended, given demographic change. But to be effective, organizations need to widen the focus of "age" from a predefined age group to all generations.

Chapter 8
Rethink Priorities: Navigating the Wise Management Agenda

Once you've grasped the importance of a Wise Management approach, you may be wondering how to go about implementing these concepts. Like climate change, the aging population and its impact on the workplace are hard for people to see and grasp. Awareness develops slowly, and the negative effects may not be obvious at first. It helps to consider the common psychological reasons behind people's reluctance to act on the threats of shifting age demographics, as they are complex and multifaceted. Several factors contribute to this inaction:[80]

Temporal Distance
One of the primary reasons for inaction is the perceived temporal distance of demographic change impacts. People tend to prioritize immediate threats over long-term ones. The aging of the workforce often feels like a distant problem, making it challenging for individuals to connect their present actions with future consequences.

Psychological Trade-Offs
Acting on demographic changes represents a trade-off between short-term and long-term benefits, which is one of the most difficult trade-offs for people to make psychologically. Immediate comfort and convenience often outweigh the perceived long-term benefits.

Uncertainty and Nonlinearity
Like climate change, the aging workforce is a nonlinear problem, meaning its effects are not always predictable or easily observable. This

---

80 https://hbr.org/2018/10/why-people-arent-motivated-to-address-climate-change

uncertainty can lead to cognitive dissonance—the disconnect between what people know about the effects of an aging workforce and their daily actions can create psychological discomfort. It also can lead to denial, as some individuals may cope with the anxiety by denying its existence or severity.

Psychological Distance

For many people, the effects of climate change, for example, feel psychologically distant. This distance can be geographical if the impacts may seem more relevant to far-off locations. The distance can be social if the consequences appear to affect others more than oneself. Or the distance can be temporal, with the most severe impacts projected for the future.

Psychological Reactance

Fear-based appeals about the demographic change sometimes backfire. Research has shown that appealing to individuals (as opposed to policy) can increase a perceived threat to personal freedom, leading to psychological reactance and resistance to change.[81]

Locus of Control

An individual's locus of control—their belief in their ability to influence outcomes—plays a role in responses to the challenge of the demographic shift in the workforce.[82] Those with an external locus of control may feel that their actions won't make a difference, leading to inaction.

Cognitive Biases

Two cognitive biases affect our perception of the likely impact of demographic change in the workplace. First, optimism bias is the tendency to believe that negative events are less likely to happen to oneself.

81   https://www.sciencedirect.com/science/article/pii/S0022103124000799
82   https://www.psychologytoday.com/intl/blog/there-is-always-another-part/201710/the-existential-dread-climate-change

Second, the status quo bias shows a preference for the current state of affairs, resisting change, even when beneficial.

Understanding these psychological factors is crucial for developing effective strategies to motivate aging workforce interventions. Approaches that bring the future mentally closer, confront uncertainty head-on, and initiate serious discussions about values among peers may help overcome these psychological barriers.

Overcoming Barriers

While these barriers exist, there are practical ways of overcoming them by focusing on the roles of the board, executive committee, line managers, and people and culture function. We will review each of these roles in detail below.

In a discussion I had recently with a group of senior executives, we all agreed that starting the conversation in the organization is key. Wise Organizations do this very deliberately. They start by acknowledging the valuable experience, stressing the benefits of multiple perspectives for innovation and problem-solving, along with the importance of institutional knowledge and experience for superior strategy execution.

A pharmaceutical company used the following team-based approach to weave in the topic of an aging workforce and link it to the business requirements: A group of R&D, production planning, and product development people joined for a meeting to scope out their business parameters and functional requirements for the next five years. On purpose, the agenda included discussing the required manpower, including alignment of experience, people skills, and an outlook of how many employees would be retiring. This formed a valuable baseline of requirements for the mid-term planning.

As a positive side effect of this meeting, this baseline provided a perfect opportunity to frame the subsequent annual discussion between managers and mature employees: Instead of falling into the same trap of "when do you want to leave, and how shall we plan your last years," the conversation explored business objectives and valued skills:

"Andrew, as you know, this is what the firm is trying to achieve and your experience is instrumental in reaching this goal. Let's talk about how this company can support you and continue to leverage your existing potential and develop it further."

For both (executive) board members and the HR community, igniting a "What if" discussion creates a healthy baseline for a mindset change and future activities. Ask something like this: "Given what we know about the demographic change, what would happen if we (as an organization) neglected to prepare in any way." Or try this approach: "What will happen if we continue to react to short-term needs (e.g., replacing a few people who are retiring) and do not focus on strategic solutions for the long term?" Make sure all stakeholders fully understand the consequences of inaction. Frame the message as tangibly as possible so that it comes alive for everyone.

Another pragmatic way to embrace a Wise Management agenda is to have leaders start talking about the innovative power of teams that blend different skills and levels of experience. Creative organizations may create a visual campaign for it. The global insurance company Allianz launched an initiative called "50 over 50" as part of its age diversity program featuring remarkable achievements of "older" employees. Tune in whenever you hear organizations talking about "Wisdom Capital," "Senior Talent," "Wise Peers," etc. Wise Organizations may spin stories to ignite a broader conversation and increase awareness even before they have a specific solution, but it is important to have a strategic plan underway and the end result in mind before you call too much attention to the program.

The Board of Directors

Wise Management ideally begins with the board of directors, but why do so many boards not take action? This depends largely on the awareness and involvement of the organization's top management. There are several reasons why an organization's board of directors may not be visibly addressing the challenges of an aging workforce:

Board Composition and Roles

Just as with the organizations themselves, it is not obvious who on the board should take responsibility for the age agenda. Technically, it should be the chair's responsibility. But when boards predefine clear roles and responsibilities, they leave little room for the accountability of a systemic challenge that spans the entire company and all its functions.

Most boards carry out their work via committees for personnel, audit, risk, technology, nomination, and sustainability. Three of these committees could be a good fit for age management:

- The personnel committee typically concerns itself with appointing members of the executive committee.
- The risk committee focuses on risk assessment and mitigation, often arising from an audit report, and evaluates the organization's risk management systems.
- The sustainability committee focuses on the environment, social dynamics, and governance to ensure the long-term viability of the firm.

Wise Management certainly has a link to social sustainability and could be addressed by this committee. But in the vast majority of organizations, sustainability efforts are focused mainly on CO_2 emissions and other environmental concerns. This emphasis leaves little room to include the aging workforce as a priority.

Often overlooked is the accountability that employee representatives have for the demographic change in the organization. They bring the collective voice of employees to top-level decision-making processes and—if done right—contribute to sustainable and strategic leadership in the organization.

Obviously, supervisory boards have a huge opportunity to shape corporate strategies in ways that align better with changing workforce demographics. They could help turn the threat of an aging workforce into an opportunity for competitive advantage by leveraging the full potential of knowledge and experience more wisely.

Lack of Awareness or Urgency

Many boards don't fully grasp the scope and urgency of aging work-force challenges. They may underestimate the impact on their organization or believe it's a future problem, rather than a present concern. Without a clear understanding of the demographic shifts and their implications, boards may not prioritize this issue.

Focus on Short-Term Metrics

Boards often concentrate on short-term financial performance and immediate business challenges. The long-term nature of aging workforce issues may not align with their typical focus on quarterly or annual results.[83] This short-term orientation can lead to neglecting strategic workforce planning.

Complexity of the Issue

Addressing an aging workforce requires a multifaceted approach involving various aspects of human resources, operations, and strategy. The complexity of developing comprehensive solutions may deter boards from tackling the issue head-on.[84] It's not a simple problem with a quick fix.

Lack of Expertise

Many board members may lack specific expertise in workforce demographics and age-related workplace issues. Without this knowledge, they may not feel equipped to address the challenges effectively or may not recognize the need to do so.

Potential for Age Discrimination Concerns

Some boards may be hesitant to openly discuss aging workforce issues due to concerns about age discrimination. They may worry that focusing on this topic could be perceived as biased against older workers.

---

83 https://www.shrm.org/foundation/aging-workforce
84 https://www.generation.org/news/meeting-the-challenges-of-an-ageing-workforce/

Insufficient Data and Metrics

Most boards rely on data to drive their decision-making. If an organization lacks robust workforce analytics or clear metrics related to aging workforce challenges, the board may not have the necessary information to recognize and address the issue.[85]

Cultural Factors

In some organizational cultures, there may be a bias toward youth and innovation that inadvertently sidelines discussions about retaining and leveraging older workers. This cultural mindset can influence board-level conversations and priorities.

Competing Priorities

Organizations have to juggle numerous challenges and opportunities. Boards may be focused on other pressing issues, such as digital transformation, market competition, or regulatory compliance, leaving less attention for demographic shifts in the workforce.[86]

The Executive Committee

Addressing the challenges of an aging workforce should be a top concern for every executive board. How can you transform the organization successfully without focusing on key characteristics of the largest and fastest growing group of any workforce? However, too often, we've seen a surprising level of reluctance from board-level leaders to put Wise Management on the agenda. There are multiple reasons why this structural challenge does not gain prominence on the executive committee's agenda, including:

– **Insufficient incentives:** Here's an interesting fact I uncovered in researching this book: I could not find any publicly listed company that offers long-term incentives for executive board members to manage demographic change successfully. There are discussions

85 https://www.aihr.com/blog/aging-workforce-challenges/
86 https://www.shrm.org/foundation/aging-workforce

of general trends and practices in long-term incentive plans, but a glaring lack of company-specific examples related to demographic change.[87] It's worth noting that some companies are beginning to tie executive bonuses to environmental, social, and governance (ESG) principles, which could potentially include demographic factors. However, no specific examples are provided in the research to date.

- **Short-term focus:** Many companies prioritize immediate business needs and short-term goals over long-term workforce planning. Wise Management requires a more strategic approach.
- **Isolated functional focus:** There is a common belief that the challenges of demographic change and the impact on organizations should be tackled by HR. It is considered to be a functional and not primarily a business problem.
- **Focus on younger talent:** Many organizations prioritize attracting and retaining younger workers, potentially overlooking the value of retaining older employees.
- **Cost perceptions:** There may be a misconception that accommodating older workers is more expensive, leading companies to deprioritize Wise Management initiatives.
- **Competing priorities:** Companies often face numerous pressing issues and limited resources, making it challenging to allocate time and budget to Wise Management initiatives.
- **Difficulty quantifying ROI:** The benefits of Wise Management can be hard to measure in the short term, making it challenging to justify the investment to stakeholders.

From my experience with a wide variety of enterprise organizations, I can say with certainty that Wise Management needs to be integrated into the overall strategy and not viewed as a separate initiative. To suc-

---

87   https://www.ey.com/content/dam/ey-unified-site/ey-com/en-in/insights/workforce/doc-uments/ey-long-term-incentive-plans-survey-report.pdf and https://www.hugessen.com/en/news/navigating-long-term-incentives-private-companies

ceed, you need to align your Wise Management practices with broader organizational goals and objectives (see Chapter 6). Then, incorporate age diversity considerations into workforce planning and talent management processes. And finally, ensure Wise Management supports key business priorities like innovation, customer service, and productivity.

We've observed that large, family-owned businesses are more likely to align Wise Management practices with their organizational goals than publicly listed ones. This is rooted in differences in their key characteristics:[88]

Key characteristics	Publicly listed	Family/privately owned
Focus and priorities	Prioritize short-term financial performance and shareholder value	Emphasize long-term sustainability, employee wellbeing, and preserving family values
Decision making	Based primarily on financial metrics and market expectations	Often consider both economic and noneconomic factors, including family dynamics and legacy
Governance and accountability	More independent directors and stricter governance structures	More family members on the board, potentially leading to less impartial decision making
Leadership style	Leaders may adopt a more formal, professional management approach	Leaders may employ a more personal, relationship-based leadership style

88 https://hbr.org/2015/04/leadership-lessons-from-great-family-businesses

Key characteristics	Publicly listed	Family/privately owned
Risk tolerance	May be more risk-averse due to shareholder scrutiny and market pressures	Might be willing to take more calculated risks for long-term growth and innovation
Stakeholder relations	Focus on a broader range of stakeholders, including shareholders, analysts, and regulators	Prioritize relationships with family members, employees, and local communities

These differences influence the executive board members' approach not only to strategy, governance, and overall business management but also to the demographic shift.

Often, publicly listed companies are much bigger than privately owned entities. The organizational size also has an effect on how well a company embraces the mindset of a Wise Organization. Ultimately, it reverts back to the respective leadership style and the prevailing culture of the company, irrespective of its size and ownership structure.

Line Managers

Being involved in the day-to-day management of people, the line manager plays an important role in navigating the demographic shift in any organization. Putting sufficient emphasis on the Wise Management topic requires the line manager to be aware of and understand its implications. The psychological aspects of the problem, as outlined earlier in this chapter, apply as well. However, the pressure of daily business and tactical considerations combined with the need to achieve short-term results will play a bigger role for the line manager, leaving little room for additional important topics. A lack of awareness across the organization can be a blocker for the respective line manager to address this subject and make it a priority. In addition, stereotyping and a belief that the problem will sort itself out at some point in the future create additional resistance.

People and Culture Leaders

The Chief P&C Officer should play a key role in putting Wise Management on the board's agenda and shaping the strategy with dedicated follow-through. However, even when you have a forward-thinking leader in the department, an outdated "human resources" mindset in the wider organization can persist, making it difficult for P&C to act strategically and proactively—particularly when faced with economic challenges.

In times of economic downturns, organizations typically deploy tools and processes that have been proven in the past to get through challenging times. Applying the principles of a Wise Organization could be seen as risky and perhaps even perceived as an additional burden, instead of a relief. But this is wrong-headed thinking; there are a number of immediate benefits to addressing age management head-on:

1. **Immediate cost savings**: Wise Management can lead to immediate reductions in age-related labor costs, such as higher engagement and preventing "drift" (see chapter 2), as well as lower sickness rates.[89]

2. **Rapid adaptation**: Older workers with the right skills can help organizations quickly adapt to changing market conditions, which is crucial during economic instability. Helping the mature workforce navigate the change and trigger their agility (encouragement to tinker with new ideas and put them into practice; to experiment and focus on continuous improvement) to leverage existing experience will foster productivity. This is essential when companies need to maximize efficiency with limited resources.[90]

89   https://cepr.org/voxeu/columns/healthy-ageing-healthy-economy
90   https://www.cedefop.europa.eu/files/3064_en.pdf

3. **Short-term productivity gains**: Investing in the health and skills of older workers can yield quick improvements in productivity, which are essential for surviving economic challenges.

4. **Immediate market responsiveness**: In sectors with an aging customer base, retaining older workers can provide an immediate advantage in understanding and responding to consumer needs.

5. **Quick resource optimization**: Wise Management allows for better utilization of existing people resources, which is critical when new hiring is limited during economic downturns[91] or when hiring freezes are in place.

6. **Intergenerational knowledge transfer**: Wise Management promotes intergenerational solidarity and knowledge-sharing, which can drive innovation and adaptability during challenging times.

7. **Retention of valuable experience**: Retaining older workers prevents the expensive loss of skills and may even increase market share. In times of economic uncertainty, preserving institutional knowledge becomes crucial for organizational resilience.

By prioritizing age management, organizations can not only weather economic challenges but also position themselves for stronger recovery and growth in the long term. As populations age, there is going to be an inevitable decline in the working-age population. This will result in a supply shortage of qualified workers, making it difficult for businesses to fill in-demand roles.[92] An organization that cannot fill crucial occupations may face declining productivity, higher labor costs, delayed business expansion, and reduced international competitiveness. If you follow the Wise Management guidelines, you won't get caught in this trap.

---

91 https://iris.who.int/bitstream/handle/10665/331978/Policy-brief-1997-8073-2019-1-eng.pdf
92 https://www.investopedia.com/articles/investing/011216/4-global-economic-issues-aging-population.asp

CHAPTER 8 SUMMARY

To pave the way to a successful age agenda, companies need to recognize the strategic importance of Wise Management in maintaining a skilled and diverse workforce. This requires senior leadership's commitment to Wise Management as a strategic priority, education about the benefits of generational diversity for better business outcomes and effective Wise Management practices, and a long-term approach to workforce planning that considers demographic trends. Organizations should develop clear business cases demonstrating the value of Wise Management initiatives and integrate Wise Management into overall human resource strategies. By addressing these challenges and prioritizing the age agenda, companies can better position themselves to harness the potential of their aging workforces and ensure long-term sustainability, innovation, and growth.

Part Three:

The Age of
Wisdom

Chapter 9
Rewrite the Silver Narrative: Age in the Context of Business Objectives

Are you ready to change the narrative around age in your company? Before you begin, keep the following two considerations in mind:

A small change in age distribution can have a big effect.

Most organizations underestimate the effect that a change in the median age has on the organization and its ability to change or transform:

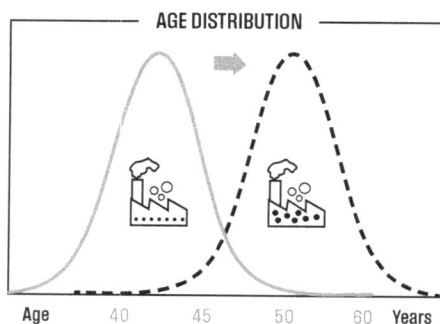

When the age distribution shifts to a higher median (an older age), by definition, more older people on average will be affected by the change or the transformation the organization is undergoing.

For example, let's say a company wants to change its way of operating from a divisional structure to an integrated matrix organization. As the age distribution shifts, more people will shift their priorities from long-term, knowledge-related goals to short-term objectives that provide immediate emotional satisfaction, according to the Social Selectivity Theory discussed in Chapter 3. Likewise, more people adapt to opportunities and constraints by regulating their goals and resources (Selection, Optimization, Compensation Theory). This has a profound impact on the successful outcome of the envisioned change process. Organizations are now faced with a two-dimensional challenge, and they typically are not even aware of it.

"Older workers" are not a homogeneous group.

Bain & Company studied the motivations and behavior of older workers and found that most fall into one of six archetypes:[1]

OPERATOR	**ARTISAN**	**STRIVER**
Looks for meaning outside work	Seeks out work that fascinates them	Wants to make something of their life
Does not seek to stand out at work	Motivated by pursuit of mastery	Motivated by status and compensation
Tends to shy away from risk	Desires autonomy	Forward planner, and often risk-averse
Often views colleagues as friends	Places lower emphasis on camaraderie	More competitive and transactional
GIVER	**EXPLORER**	**PIONEER**
Finds meaning in helping others	Values freedom and experiences	On a mission to change the world
Least motivated by money	Craves variety and autonomy	Autonomous and risk-tolerant
Strong team spirit	Willing to trade security for flexibility	Identify profoundly with their work
Values personal growth and learning	Less motivated by status	Vision is often at least partially altruistic

Source: Bain & Company

1   https://www.bain.com/insights/better-with-age-the-rising-importance-of-older-workers/

Your future Wise Management activities will have to align with each of these archetypes. Also note, these archetypes are not equally distributed. As people age, a disproportionate number of them become Artisans and Givers. Artisans value autonomy and look for meaningful work. They are motivated primarily by mastering their craft. For Givers, work is about service. They feel rewarded when their actions make a positive impact on other people's lives.

As workers age, more of them become Artisans and Givers

Share of each archetype, by age

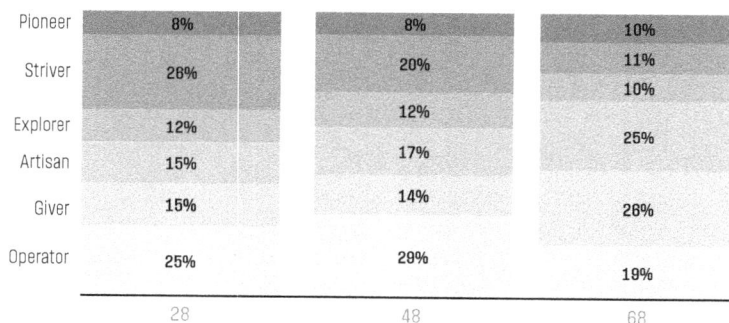

	28	48	68
Pioneer	8%	8%	10%
Striver	26%	20%	11%
			10%
Explorer	12%	12%	25%
Artisan	15%	17%	
Giver	15%	14%	28%
Operator	25%	29%	19%

Note: Respondents from US, Germany, France, Italy, Japan, Australia, Canada, Finland, Denmark, Norway, Saudi Arabia, Sweden, UK, and UAE

Source: Bain Worker Survey (n = 27,700)

With these two truths in mind, let's dive in. For an effective way to ensure that your Wise Management initiative is linked to your corporate objectives and strategy, use the following tool. Although this template was originally developed for CEOs,[2] I've adapted it to apply to the challenge of planning around an aging workforce. This question-

---

2   Adapted from McKinsey's CEO's essentials Checklist: https://www.mckinsey.com/capabilities/strategy-and-corporate-finance/our-insights/the-ceos-essential-checklist-questions-every-chief-executive-should-be-able-to-answer#/

naire will help to evaluate your current situation, so you can better understand where to focus your efforts and where to continue expanding existing strengths. Simply rate your answers on the basis of the following list.

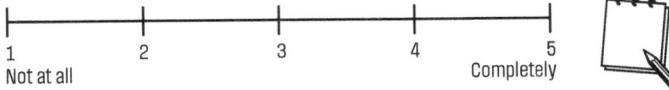

1   2   3   4   5
Not at all   Completely

1. **Direction Setting**
   - **Organizational vision:** How well-defined and widely communicated is your organization's vision of success, particularly among your experienced employees?
   - **Competitive strategy:** What strategic initiatives have you developed to leverage your seasoned workforce's expertise, allowing you to gain a competitive edge in the market?
   - **Resource management and workforce utilization:** To what extent have you realigned your budget, human capital, and other resources to support your key business objectives? Additionally, how effectively are you capitalizing on the wealth of knowledge and experience possessed by your employees aged 50 and above?

2. **Organizational Alignment Shifts:**
   How well does your evolving organizational culture align with both your strategic goals and the changing demographics of your workforce?
   - **Organizational structure and adaptability:** Is your current organizational design striking the right balance between stability and flexibility to optimize execution speed and effectiveness? Are you seeing any signs of imbalance resulting from unaddressed demographic changes within your company?
   - **Talent management and generational transition:** Have you

placed the most suitable individuals in your highest-impact roles? Considering the ongoing retirement of Baby Boomers and Generation X employees, is your leadership pipeline robust enough to ensure continuity and future success?

3. **Leadership Mobilization**
   - **Leadership skills and experience:** Does your senior leadership team possess a diverse range of complementary abilities that align with the necessary expertise and experience levels required for your aging organization?
   - **Effective management processes:** Has your senior leadership team established a well-structured annual workflow and regular business evaluation schedule to ensure smooth operations, particularly considering the evolving demographics of your workforce?

4. **Board Engagement**
   - **Regarding relationships and trust:** How effectively have you fostered a climate of openness and mutual respect with the board? Have you demonstrated full transparency and actively sought their perspectives, particularly concerning the ongoing demographic changes?
   - **Concerning director capabilities and involvement:** Are you providing adequate training and development opportunities for your board members? Have you been proactive in identifying and leveraging their individual strengths and expertise to benefit the aging organization?

5. **Personal Effectiveness**
   - **Leadership authenticity and adaptability:** How well do your leaders balance staying true to their core principles while flexibly adapting their leadership style to meet evolving organizational needs, particularly those arising from an increasingly

mature workforce?

- **Servant leadership and continuous growth:** To what extent do you embody a humble, service-oriented leadership approach that prioritizes the success of others? How effectively are you enhancing your capabilities to support and maximize the potential of your experienced employees?

6. **External Stakeholder Connection and Alignment**
   - **Interactions:** Do you fully understand your stakeholders' needs, and can you find constructive common ground with them? If your stakeholders want you to be innovative, are you doing enough to retain and leverage institutional knowledge?
   - **Moments of truth:** Have you built resilience ahead of any potential crisis, so that you will be able to mitigate the impact and use adversity to unlock opportunities? For example, are you shaping your employer brand to be attractive to both younger as well as older potential employees?

7. **Crisis Preparedness and Opportunity Recognition**
   - To what extent have you developed organizational resilience in anticipation of any potential crises? In what ways are you proactively shaping your employer brand to appeal to a diverse workforce, including both younger and more experienced professionals?

By answering these questions and thoroughly discussing the outcomes and ramifications, you'll create a valuable baseline from which you can start design the blueprint for a Wise Organization.

CHAPTER 9 SUMMARY

It is paramount to link Wise Management to corporate objectives. An important prerequisite is to fully understand how well your organization stacks up against the requirements for a Wise Organization. Recognize that you will change your age narrative successfully only if you focus on achieving your business objectives first: How will an aging workforce that is not a homogeneous, but an experienced talent group, contribute to achieving those objectives in the best way possible? Any actions that follow will contribute to changing the age narrative.

Chapter 10
Architect a Wise Organization: Blueprint for Success

In Chapter 3, we defined Wise Management as a strategic approach to orchestrating the inevitable demographic shift that combines the needs of aging workers with a focus on their integration into and role in a multigenerational workforce. This effort is about recognizing, incorporating, and leveraging age-related differences and unique strengths in the organization for the benefit of the company and the wellbeing of the aging individual.

As you apply these principles, you will shape your company step-by-step into a Wise Organization. The path to success focuses on five key elements: Organization, Leaders, People, Processes, and Culture/Mindset.

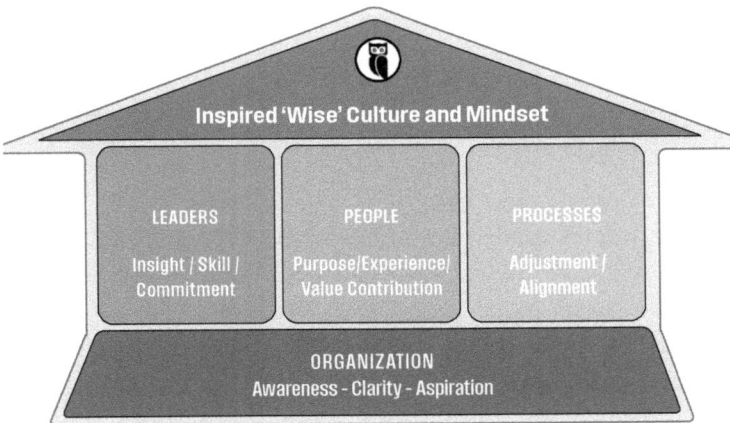

Inspired 'Wise' Culture and Mindset

LEADERS	PEOPLE	PROCESSES
Insight / Skill / Commitment	Purpose/Experience/ Value Contribution	Adjustment / Alignment

ORGANIZATION
Awareness - Clarity - Aspiration

© WiseForce Advisors

This model is designed with a single objective: To unleash the potential of 50+ workers to drive innovation, transformation, and growth. This approach is rooted in social and behavioral science, as well as the latest insights in neuroscience, in addition to first-hand insights and experience from our specialized consulting work with many valued clients. When it's done right, this process helps organizations and their employees experience a new level of performance, productivity, and satisfaction.

It is paramount to understand that these five elements are interlinked, and you have to put a considerable amount of energy into each area to realize the vision of building a Wise Organization. The journey starts with looking closely at your organization to get clarity on your business strategy and develop a sense of how a Wise Management approach will help you execute the plan, each step of the way.

Organization: Awareness—Clarity—Aspiration

Purpose and Strategic Alignment

I have seen many companies impulsively take action to improve their age management stance; yet in each case, a missing link to the organization's overarching goals and business strategy caused their actions to be perceived as nice to have, but not imperative to the future success of the company.

To assure the appropriate attention and necessary impact, start by making sure you are clear about your organization's strategic direction: Consider your vision (the long-term aspiration and your source of inspiration and motivation for employees and stakeholders) and mission (definition of your organization's current purpose and approach), as well as the goals you want to achieve, in what time frame, and with what resources.

Next, reflect on any current initiatives, programs, transformation agenda, or change mandate. And, finally, revisit your People and Culture strategy, considering whether it's capable of supporting the organization in achieving its business goals. With alignment across vision, goals, and resources, you can begin to anchor the Wise Management mindset into your strategy execution.

This concept will be new to many people in your organization, so it is important to start creating awareness of the subject in general and the impact of the changing age distribution on the company strategy. Communicating early and often will allow you to involve a larger number of people in the age management process and to continue the momentum once the initiative is underway.

Raising Awareness

As explained in earlier chapters, you'll likely be confronting a long list of age-based stereotypes as you undertake the age management imperative. The most effective way to raise awareness is to put this topic on the agenda everywhere, starting with the executive board. Effective ways to spark an interest in the subject include:

1. **Providing data, conducting workforce assessments:** Use tools to analyze the number of workers approaching retirement age and potential impacts on knowledge, expertise, and productivity.

2. **Sharing age-related statistics:** Present evidence demonstrating the benefits of employing and investing in older workers to line managers, supervisory staff, and the general workforce.

3. **Organizing workshops, seminars, or coffee talks over lunch:** Hold educational events focused on age management issues and the value of experience.

4. **Discussing the option of launching intergenerational mentoring programs:** Encourage knowledge-sharing between older and younger employees to foster mutual understanding and respect, and test the appetite of the audience.

5. **Creating an interactive internal careers page:** Showcase opportunities aligned with older employees' goals and highlight their potential contributions.

6. **Establishing Employee Resource Groups (ERGs):** Create dedicated spaces to discuss and celebrate age diversity and inclusion.
7. **Using internal communication channels:** Share resources, educational opportunities, and inclusive stories related to age diversity.
8. **Conducting pulse surveys:** Gather feedback on age-related issues and perceptions within the organization.
9. **Inviting guest speakers:** Ask age management experts to talk about this subject and present an outside perspective.
10. **Highlighting success stories:** Showcase examples of older workers' contributions and achievements within the organization.

By focusing on what is possible, rather than what is wrong, these activities will create an emotional baseline and a readiness to talk about the subject in much broader ways. And since the executive board advises direct reports to put important topics on their agendas, starting at the top ensures that age management makes its way throughout the organization. By implementing these strategies, organizations can raise awareness about the aging workforce and its implied potential for both the organization and the individual.

After you've created initial awareness, it's time to get clarity on the way forward. At this point, it's critical to choose a systematic approach for thoroughly diagnosing the status quo.

Running an Organizational Diagnostic

Before you start the diagnostic process, select the right stakeholders and participants—and remember, the primary role of Wise Management is to support your business strategy.

A next consideration is to define stakeholder expectation and involvement. As a general recommendation, choose stakeholders not only for the diagnostic phase but also for the subsequent implementation phases. You'll want to anticipate the potential outcome of the diagnostic process and which areas or functions may be affected. This stakeholder group may include leaders or representatives of business lines, geographies, functions, other subject matter experts, or simply individuals whose opinions are valued. Keep in mind that stakeholders who have not been involved in the diagnostic, but are affected by its results, may question the diagnostic process and outcome, and they will be less motivated to help with the subsequent implementation phase.

Visible senior management involvement sends a strong signal to the organization, underlining the importance of this endeavor. It's not a nice-to-have exercise, but rather a necessary step to achieve high-priority business goals.

An important stakeholder group to consider is members of the works council. They provide an important and often complementary view, which can lead to a broader discussion.

Last but not least, the People and Culture function plays an important role in this process, as described in Chapter 6. In most cases, P&C also can be tasked with leading the diagnostic process.

After you've identified the main stakeholders, you're ready to consider what data to look at and how to analyze and draw conclusions from the available information. Organizations could look at the following data sources:

General Workforce Data
- Conduct a comprehensive workforce demographic analysis.[3]
- Draw from existing engagement surveys.
- Identify potential skills gaps and knowledge transfer needs.[4]
- Assess health and ergonomic considerations for older workers.[5]
- Analyze productivity trends across different age groups.[6]

3   https://pubdata.leuphana.de/bitstream/20.500.14123/687/1/Diss_2021_Wilckens_Max-_R_Organizational.pdf
4   https://pubdata.leuphana.de/bitstream/20.500.14123/687/1/Diss_2021_Wilckens_Max-_R_Organizational.pdf
5   https://pmc.ncbi.nlm.nih.gov/articles/PMC11200061/
6   https://www.econstor.eu/bitstream/10419/302079/1/16-ENTRENOVA-2023.pdf

- Review retirement patterns and intentions among older employees.[7]
- Analyze HR data on performance, absenteeism, and turnover rates by age cohorts.[8]

Data Pointing to Awareness

- Assess the current organizational climate and practices related to age inclusivity.[9]
- Assess the awareness of the potential impact that aging employees have on the bottom line.
- Evaluate the awareness of mature workers' having unique needs and changing values.
- Assess the sensitivity of intergenerational interaction in the company.
- To what degree is "age" a part of the organization's diversity, equity, and inclusion initiatives?

Talent Management Processes and Policies

- Evaluate existing HR policies and practices for age-friendliness.[10]
- Assess the availability of alternative career paths to better leverage the potential of the mature employee.
- Examine the organization's leadership approach to age diversity.[11]
- Evaluate current training (upskilling and reskilling) and development programs for age inclusiveness.[12]
- Examine the hiring policies and aligned criteria on age.

---

7   https://pubdata.leuphana.de/bitstream/20.500.14123/687/1/Diss_2021_Wilckens_Max-_R_Organizational.pdf
8   https://www.econstor.eu/bitstream/10419/302079/1/16-ENTRENOVA-2023.pdf
9   https://pubdata.leuphana.de/bitstream/20.500.14123/687/1/Diss_2021_Wilckens_Max-_R_Organizational.pdf
10 http://fox.leuphana.de/portal/files/22035480/repo_15387880_oa_byncnd.pdf
11 http://fox.leuphana.de/portal/files/22035480/repo_15387880_oa_byncnd.pdf
12 https://pubdata.leuphana.de/bitstream/20.500.14123/687/1/Diss_2021_Wilckens_Max-_R_Organizational.pdf

- Analyze job designs and work arrangements for flexibility and accommodation.[13]
- Evaluate the degree of age-inclusive language on the organization's website.
- Evaluate the encouragement of working in mixed-aged teams.
- Evaluate reverse mentoring programs.
- Examine the effectiveness of knowledge transfer processes.
- Evaluate retirement policies (phased, early, others options).

Attitudes and Beliefs

- Assess various degrees of unconscious bias. (Do managers presume that older workers are change-adverse, expensive, have difficulties adapting and learning, or cause health-related absenteeism to go up?)
- Assess evidence of career derailers for older employees in the company.
- Assess evidence of negative age stereotypes in the organization, which can create a climate of age discrimination.
- Assess the organization's focus on opportunities: As the workforce ages, there's generally a decrease in employees' focus on future opportunities at work. However, a positive Organizational Climate for Successful Aging (OCSA) can buffer this negative relationship, particularly for older employees.[14]

Index Tools to Harness Complexity

A few years ago, Deller *et al.* (2018) presented a tool named the "Silver Work Index (SWI)," designed to help organizations evaluate their capabilities in employing older workers.[15] The SWI index comprises elements of organizational culture, leadership, and specific human

13   https://www.frontiersin.org/journals/psychology/articles/10.3389/fpsyg.2024.1439271/pdf
14   https://www.frontiersin.org/journals/psychology/articles/10.3389/fpsyg.2016.01007/full
15   https://pmc.ncbi.nlm.nih.gov/articles/PMC11200061/#ref-38

resources (HR) practices which are conceptually defined but yet to be operationalized for usage as an assessment tool.

To bridge gaps in the measurement of organizational practices related to aging at work, Wilckens *et al.* (2020) proposed a comprehensive, multifaceted, and thoroughly conceptualized measure of organizational practices related to aging at work, the Later Life Workplace Index (LLWI).[16] Through the course of four articles, the LLWI is developed based on qualitative interview data, operationalized, validated based on multiple field studies among older workers, and applied in a multilevel study among older employees of 101 organizations.

Results suggest that organizational practices are not uniform, but multifaceted in their presence within organizations and their effects for the employment of older workers. The LLWI distinguishes nine domains of practices, including an age-friendly organizational climate, work design, individual development, and practices for tailoring the retirement transition. In this way, it provides a foundation for more granular organizational-level research in the field.[17]

Attempts to validate these two indices, however, (and the degree of readiness among companies for the aging workforce trend) revealed country-specific variances due to differences in laws and regulations that complicated definition, comparison, and standardization.[18]

What Should the Process of Data Gathering and Evaluation Look Like?

Given that the challenge of an aging workforce is a growing concern in many organizations, but levels of experience in managing such a shift are limited, we propose a pragmatic approach to the diagnostic, involving suitable stakeholders in both data gathering and evaluation. This will increase the engagement level and commitment for future involvement.

16 https://pmc.ncbi.nlm.nih.gov/articles/PMC11200061/#ref-115
17 https://pubdata.leuphana.de/bitstream/20.500.14123/687/1/Diss_2021_Wilckens_Max-_R_Organizational.pdf
18 https://pmc.ncbi.nlm.nih.gov/articles/PMC11200061/#S3

Based on our experience with companies in many different industries, we suggest gathering data from the following four areas to assure a multilevel perspective, expert knowledge, cost-effectiveness, large and customizable sample sizes, company-specific concerns through stakeholder interviews, and insights from existing employee data:

1. Existing Workforce Data (conclusions from aggregate)	3. Stakeholder Interviews (company-specific concerns for strategy implementation)
2. HR Focus Group (expert insight)	4. Wise Management Effectiveness Survey (insights from employees)

The advantage of a multi-dimensional setup is potentially higher employee engagement. When employees see tangible changes later resulting from their input, it creates a sense of empowerment and ownership. This, in turn, has a positive effect on how well a Wise Management approach supports the firm's strategy implementation and goal achievement.

Existing Workforce Data, as outlined earlier in this chapter, typically provides individual (and often disconnected) data points. But you'll want to draw conclusions from an aggregate view across the entire data set. Here's an example of how this comes into play:

The executive board of a large insurance company asked Peter, the HR director, to look at the company's recent engagement score data to find out whether the organization "has a problem with the 55+ cohort." Peter's data showed higher rates of engagement (with a Net Promoter Score of +10) in the 55- to 65-year-old bracket. Peter eagerly reported back to the board, stating, "We do not have a problem with our older workforce."

In the absence of a broader data analysis, however—combined with a lack of understanding of the entire issue—Peter's company was misguided. If he'd formed an aggregate view across a number of data sources, he would have seen that willingness to participate in training decreased as people in the firm aged and that this cohort was taking advantage of early retirement options at a disproportionately high rate. With this view, Peter would have gone back to the board with a different message, such as:

"Our employees in their late-stage careers seem to be focusing on the early exit option, with less interest in learning new things. Maybe they are engaging with new initiatives simply due to a subconscious desire not to rock the boat any longer."

The **HR Focus Group** is an effective way of gathering data about observations, concerns, and missed opportunities. It's best to limit the focus group to eight to 12 participants, ensuring a diverse representation of specialization, tenure, and demographics. Define the purpose and specific goals of the focus group beforehand to ensure that the discussions remain focused and productive. A skilled, neutral facilitator should guide discussions and encourage an open dialogue, so that all participants have the opportunity to contribute.

It is particularly important that the focus group aims to generate data and not solve a problem. This is particularly important because, in many organizations, participating in such a focus group will be the first opportunity to discuss the challenges of an aging workforce more systematically—and participants may be inclined to jump to conclusions quickly.

Stakeholder Interviews should be conducted by a neutral interviewer. Depending on the size of the organization, aim for seven to 15 interviews across a range of roles and functions. These structured interviews can cover the same topics as the HR Focus Group.

Finally, the **Wise Management Effectiveness Survey** is a proprietary tool, conducted by a WiseForce Advisors expert, to assess key factors such as awareness and culture, processes and policies, unconscious bias, leadership, and senior stakeholder involvement.

The Wise Management Mirror Workshop Effect

The final step of the diagnostic is to interpret the data and create a plan going forward. We recommend a team workshop exercise with participants selected from among the people who contributed to the preceding data gathering process. The idea is to hold up a mirror and look into the data. It is a "What are we saying about ourselves?" kind of exercise.

The mirror workshop is based on the principle that team members can gain valuable insights by seeing themselves, a challenge, or an opportunity through their colleagues' eyes. This approach fosters trust, enhances self-awareness, and strengthens the commitment for subsequent action.[19]

During this workshop, the objective is to align on the importance of the senior workforce for the execution of the corporate strategy. You're going to build a collective understanding of the data messages (results) and build consensus on the "drive factors" that could accelerate your performance and the "drag factors" that hold you back. Encourage debate to identify the key themes and priority areas that emerge from the data, then have a frank dialogue to assign ownership for the results. End the session with clarity on next steps and commitment to achieving them.

The Magic of the Mirror Walks

In this workshop, participants analyze data and draw conclusions following a process that addresses emotional, cognitive, behavioral, and social dimensions. Accordingly, they are asked to answer certain questions as they walk in pairs or groups of three and look at the data.

---

19   https://better-teams.com/the-mirror-activity-team-building-foster-trust/

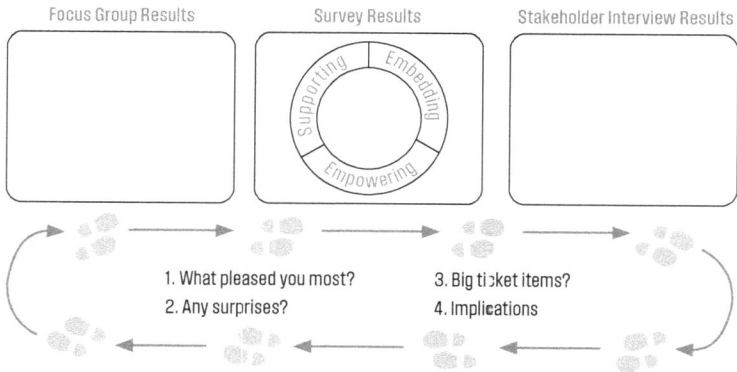

Focus Group Results   Survey Results   Stakeholder Interview Results

1. What pleased you most?
2. Any surprises?
3. Big ticket items?
4. Implications

Each question focuses attention on a particular data set, situation, or challenge. First, each participant goes through a reflection and discovery phase, by looking at the data individually and concluding, what pleases, what surprises, and what general themes surface with what implications.

Following the self-discovery step is a peer-exchange and feedback loop to identify areas where perceptions differ. Pairs of participants reflect on the insights gained from others' perspectives. Subsequently, plenary discussions aggregate the views from each group.

The workshop proceeds with many such "mirror walks," using different pair groupings and different questions to trigger diversity of thought and perspectives. This facilitator-led discussion is a delicate process that brings the most appropriate and relevant focus areas to light.

Because we are human, we interpret things differently, have different biases, and are subject to different influences. To avoid potential confusion, frustration, or incongruence between say/do, a subsequent team alignment diagnostic is important to create the desired baseline. In this step, workshop participants will aim to align on a handful of core topics.

The final step is to agree on next steps, specific actions, and clear accountability. Here's how we see this play out in practice: Organizations that have finished the diagnostic phase but neglect to keep the momentum going to build on these insights will fail. This is why it is good practice to plan follow-up meetings with senior stakeholders before kicking off the diagnostic process.

The main purpose of these follow-up meetings is to convert the findings into an implementation plan.

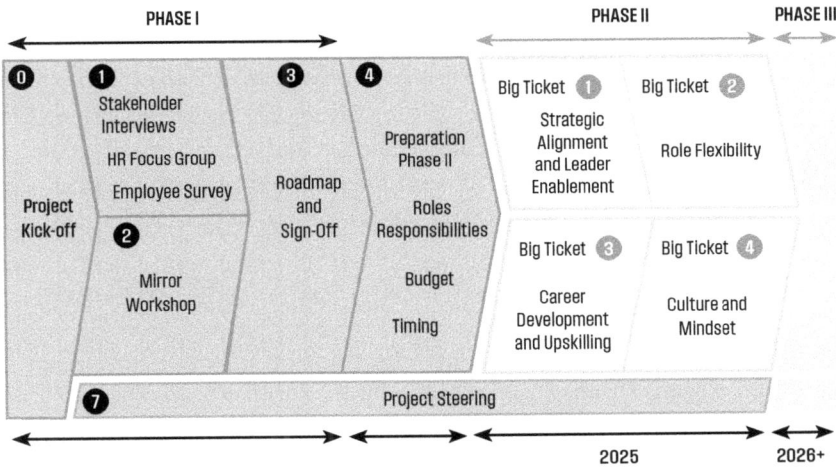

The conceptual framework of the mirror workshop provides a structured approach for teams to gain valuable insights through reflection and peer feedback, ultimately fostering a more cohesive and high-performing team environment and performance. The mirror workshop exposes the status quo and identifies what actions are needed to support the overarching strategy implementation.

Aspiration and Importance of Keeping Alignment when Executing the Strategy

A final word on setting your aspirations for the organization appropriately high: Wise Management—defined earlier in this book as "a new strategic approach to **recognize, incorporate and leverage** age-related differences and unique strengths for the benefit of both the organization and the aging individual"—will play a significant role in the execution of your business strategy. It affects at least one-fourth of your workforce, so aim high and commit the time and energy to do it right.

Above all, avoid the following pitfalls, which often impede strategy execution alignment, and which also are relevant for the Wise Management agenda:

Communication and clarity: Ineffective communication of strategic goals causes misalignment across the organization. When employees lack a clear understanding of the strategy, it becomes difficult to tie their efforts to the overall objectives. To avoid information silos between departments that can further hinder the flow of crucial information needed for coordinated execution, assure consistent and thorough communication.

Cultural resistance: Resistance to change is a significant obstacle in strategy execution. Employees and management may be averse to new initiatives, due to fear of the unknown or comfort with the status quo. Be aware that ingrained practices and longstanding organizational habits can be particularly challenging to overcome ("we have always done it this way" vs. inviting constructive feedback and innovative solutions).

Resource allocation: Remember that inadequate resource allocation can severely hamper strategy execution. Ensure sufficient funding, personnel, or technology to support strategic initiatives; be aware of limited budgets and tight timelines as well as skills gaps within the workforce that require significant investment in training and development.

Alignment and coordination: Every department and team should move in sync with the strategy. Ensure alignment to avoid various parts of the organization operating in isolation, conflicting priorities and miscommunication arising, and resources being wasted, ultimately derailing strategy execution.

Performance monitoring and evaluation: Inadequate monitoring and evaluation processes hinder execution, too. Apply appropriate performance metrics to assess the effectiveness of execution[20] and assure robust feedback mechanisms.

Organizational structure: Make sure that the organization's structure itself supports the strategy focus. Assure that budgeting and operations are aligned with the strategy, and that operational plans are adapted to include the current focus.[21]

By addressing these challenges, organizations can align their actions with their aspirations.

Leaders

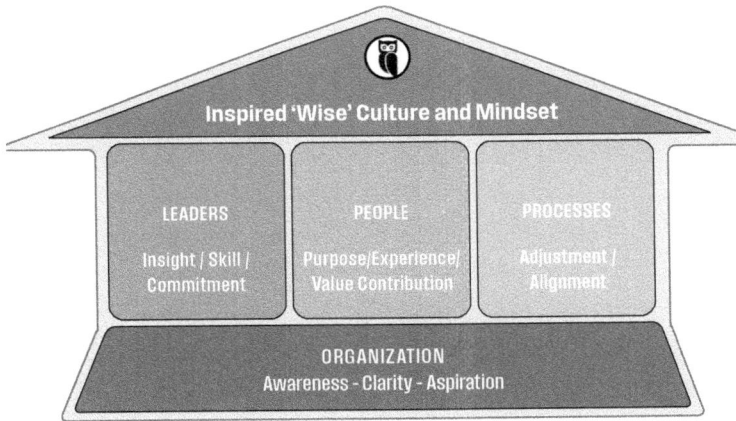

Inspired 'Wise' Culture and Mindset

LEADERS	PEOPLE	PROCESSES
Insight / Skill / Commitment	Purpose/Experience/ Value Contribution	Adjustment / Alignment

ORGANIZATION
Awareness - Clarity - Aspiration

© WiseForce Advisors

Leaders always play a crucial role in supporting their teams, regardless of age. However, it is becoming increasingly difficult for leaders to manage the unfolding generational divide. Signs of this divide include:[22]

20 https://www.kpimegalibrary.com/blog/strategy-alignment
21 https://balancedscorecard.org/blog/common-risks-and-challenges-impacting-strategy-execution/
22 https://www.shiftbase.com/glossary/generational-diversity

- **Communication style differences:** Older generations prefer face-to-face or phone communication, while younger generations favor digital channels like instant messaging and emails.
- **Varying work values:** Different generations prioritize different aspects of work, such as work-life balance, job security, or meaningful work opportunities.
- **Stereotypes and biases:** Older employees may be seen as resistant to change, while younger ones might be perceived as lacking experience or commitment.
- **Engagement disparities:** A stark contrast exists in engagement rates, with 71 percent of Millennials not engaged at work, compared to 35 percent of Baby Boomers.
- **Conflicting preferences for work arrangements:** Nearly 40 percent of employees aged 18–34 prefer remote work, while 71 percent of Baby Boomers favor traditional office routines.

Wise Management Leadership Training

The demographic shift in organizations presents an unprecedented challenge for the leaders involved—one that calls for dedicated support and bespoke leadership training. The overarching objective of the training will be to achieve more effective management of the over-50 workforce for more sustainable goal achievement. This curriculum has to address the challenges of managing a widening generational divide conceptually, as well on an individual leader level. And it should include a focus on managing age-diverse teams as well as hands-on guidance for how to manage intergenerational dynamics.[23]

Important outcomes of Wise Management leadership training might include:
- raising awareness and closing knowledge gaps
- recognizing and avoiding risks ("bias" and "drift")

---

23 https://www.reedtalentsolutions.com/articles/challenges-and-opportunities-of-the-ageing-workforce

- learning new management instruments (processes and tools) and increasing effectiveness
- managing change more successfully with new tools

To implement new insights after the training, leaders can set the tone for inclusion by promoting age diversity as a valuable asset to the organization, challenging age-related stereotypes and biases, and implementing and enforcing anti-discrimination policies. By actively championing age diversity, leaders can foster an environment in which older workers feel valued and respected.

Leaders will also play a vital role in promoting ongoing development. They should prioritize technology training for older workers,[24] support tailored learning programs that cater to older workers' learning styles, and encourage knowledge sharing between generations. By investing in continuous learning, leaders help older workers (and the organization as a whole) stay current and engaged in their roles.

Heads of departments and functions can enhance job satisfaction for older workers by designing complex and meaningful roles that leverage experience,[25] creating clear pathways for career advancement,[26] and offering opportunities for mentoring younger colleagues.

All of these strategies can help older workers feel purposeful and valued in their positions.

How about fostering supportive relationships at work? Leaders can cultivate a supportive work environment by encouraging social connections and teamwork across age groups, organizing events and activities that promote intergenerational bonding, and embedding older workers in networks of warm, trusting relationships.[27] This social support can increase motivation and facilitate informal learning opportunities.

24 https://sloanreview.mit.edu/article/how-tech-fails-late-career-workers/
25 https://sloanreview.mit.edu/article/how-tech-fails-late-career-workers/
26 https://www.wtsenergy.com/attracting-and-retaining-older-workers-this-is-how-it-is-done/
27 https://sloanreview.mit.edu/article/how-tech-fails-late-career-workers/

Effective leaders will also acknowledge the contributions of older workers, for example, by implementing recognition programs that highlight the unique value of experienced workers,[28] promoting senior employees to showcase their expertise,[29] and celebrating the achievements and milestones of older workers. Recognition helps boost morale and reinforces the importance of older workers to the organization.

Most importantly, leaders can support older workers if they lead by example and hire/promote older individuals into leadership roles,[30] demonstrate a personal commitment to age diversity, and actively seek input and advice from experienced team members.

To further build on the insights from your Wise Management leadership training, consider these additional roles for leaders in your organization, emphasizing the following:

Providing Career Development Opportunities
- Offer leadership roles and advancement paths for experienced workers.
- Provide opportunities to take on mentoring or advisory positions.
- Support lateral moves to leverage skills in new areas.

Addressing Financial Concerns
- Offer competitive compensation that recognizes experience.
- Provide robust retirement planning resources and support.
- Consider offering phased retirement options.

Redesigning Job Roles
- Create positions that leverage the experience of seasoned employees.

---

28 https://zenohealthgroup.com/7-essential-strategies-to-activate-an-ageing-workforce/
29 https://www.wtsenergy.com/attracting-and-retaining-older-workers-this-is-how-it-is-done/
30 https://recruitingdaily.com/how-to-best-support-older-workers/

- Offer project-based or consulting roles for those seeking reduced hours.
- Use technology to reduce physically demanding tasks where possible.

Fostering an Inclusive Culture
- Celebrate the contributions and achievements of older workers.
- Encourage social connections across age groups.
- Seek input from older employees on workplace policies and practices.

To further strengthen the impact of Wise Management, leaders should prioritize strategies for managing generational divides and enhancing leadership effectiveness:

Managing generational divides	Enhancing leadership effectiveness
Be aware of different communication preferences and avoid miscommunication.	Leverage existing experience and knowledge of your mature workforce.
Balance potentially conflicting career and work-life expectations.	Rework and align incentive systems with corporate objectives.
Address unconscious bias for the benefit of effective collaboration.	Help younger leaders refine their leadership approach toward older employees
Bridge intergenerational challenges arising from rapid technological changes.	Blend the needs of an aging workforce with corporate requirements.
Be conscious of diverse motivational factors that drive engagement in different age groups.	Provide and actively support continued career development opportunities.

In conclusion, leadership plays a multifaceted and critical role in supporting older workers. Through their actions and policies, leaders can create an environment where older workers thrive, contribute their valuable experience, and remain engaged and productive members of the workforce—playing an instrumental role in achieving the company's objectives.

People

© WiseForce Advisors

In Chapter 3, we outlined how the Life Stage Theory, along with the Selection, Optimization, and Compensation (SOC) model and the Socioemotional Selectivity Theory (SST), helps to explain changes in decision-making and behavioral patterns as people age. Older employees typically reach a point at which they reflect on their experience and job fulfillment. Intrinsically, they seek clarity on their late-stage career goals, and they long for a repurposing of their work contributions.

This can be a lonely situation for the employee who is questioning their role and value to the organization they have served for years. The process requires introspection and reflection, but how does it begin? The individual may first look to see what options the organization provides and wonder, "Is my boss the right person to approach? Or am I seen as a potential candidate for the next workforce reduction plan?" To someone in this position, a late-stage career development plan may feel like a surprisingly new concept.

In an ideal and wisely managed company, leadership will have gone through training as described in the previous chapter. In this case, the employee's manager could look for opportunities to initiate this conversation proactively. However, although many managers will be empathetic and capable of great leadership, I do not recommend that 50+ workers discuss all of the intricacies of their late-stage career phase only with their direct supervisor. The process addresses personal questions and sensitive topics that will affect their working relationship going forward. Furthermore, it requires special psychological and conceptual knowledge, superior coaching, and facilitation skills that the manager may not have, even if basic training has been provided.

The Catalyst Program

The WiseForce Advisors Catalyst Program is a customized learning modality designed specifically for people over the age of 50. It is a blended program designed to encourage a mindset change around future work contributions and impact, including our proprietary assessment and a reflective inquiry process, followed by coaching and sustained learning via tailored push content.

The Catalyst Program links age-related behavioural change to productivity gain

---

1. START & ASSESS

Self-Assessment

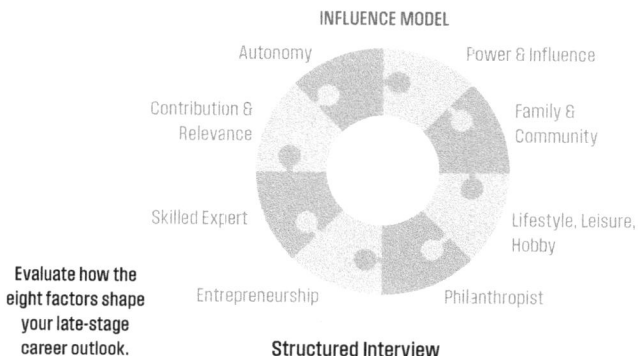

INFLUENCE MODEL

Autonomy

Power & Influence

Contribution & Relevance

Family & Community

Skilled Expert

Lifestyle, Leisure, Hobby

Evaluate how the eight factors shape your late-stage career outlook.

Entrepreneurship

Philanthropist

Structured Interview

---

2. REFLECT & GROW

Personal Navigator Workshop

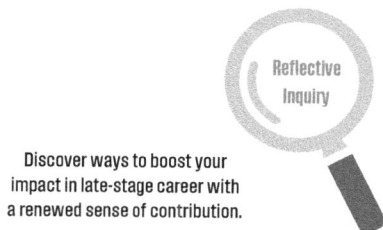

Reflective Inquiry

Discover ways to boost your impact in late-stage career with a renewed sense of contribution.

---

3. IMPLEMENT & GAIN

Implement your impact plan with renewed purpose for greater engagement and productivity.

Milestone

Milestone

Milestone

Milestone

IMPACT PLAN

Insights and committed action summarized in impact plan

The purpose of this intervention is to reinvigorate mature talent with a new sense of purpose and work contribution, and to promote higher levels of engagement and sustained productivity. We've seen a wide range of participants gain valuable insights from this program and use this information to shape their late-stage career phase within their employers' organizations.

Years ago, when I had just finished designing the Catalyst Program and discussed the intended opportunity and impact with the first prospects, a client I approached was skeptical but open to running a pilot intervention with only two participants (when a more suitable number would have been between 10 and 15 participants). I learned that the two participants were longtime employees of the company, visibly not engaged, and critical toward anything new.

I agreed to run the pilot for just these two individuals. We completed the first step, a self-assessment, and then moved on to the Navigator Workshop. At the end of the workshop, I asked each of them to draw a personal symbol, summarizing an important insight and takeaway, and how they envisioned their purpose and value contribution in the company going forward. Both men—close to their 60th birthdays—presented their drawings to each other at the same time. Much to my surprise, each of them had drawn a red heart.

That moment represented a complete turnaround from our first interactions. Clearly, the intervention had touched each of them at a deeper level, triggering a desire to be recognized as human beings and appreciated as colleagues who had more to offer the organization. I had touched on their desire to be reconnected to a deeper sense of purpose and belonging. Since the launch of this program, I've had many similar experiences, but this first one holds a special place in my heart.

Theory U

At its core, the Catalyst Program leverages the principles of Otto Scharmer's Theory U model. Scharmer is a senior lecturer at the Massachusetts Institute of Technology (MIT) and the founding chair of the Presencing Institute. His 2009 book, *Theory U: Leading from the Future as It Emerges*, presents a framework, a method, and a way of being for transformative change that focuses on shifting collective awareness and intention, so we can connect to the more authentic or higher aspects of ourselves.

Scharmer proposes that the quality of results in any social system is a function of the quality of awareness or consciousness of its participants.[31] Accordingly, the core principle of Theory U is to shift from ego-system awareness to ecosystem awareness, encouraging people to see the whole as part of the whole and make decisions based on the interconnectedness of all things.[32] This approach aims to break through past unproductive patterns of behavior and enable individuals and organizations to create innovative solutions for the future.[33]

Theory U is represented by a U-shaped process that moves through several stages:[34]

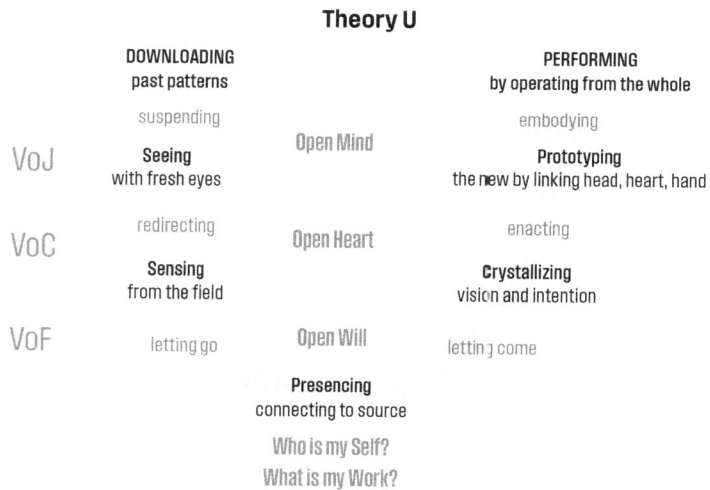

Theory U

	DOWNLOADING past patterns			PERFORMING by operating from the whole
VoJ	suspending	Open Mind		embodying
	Seeing with fresh eyes			**Prototyping** the new by linking head, heart, hand
VoC	redirecting	Open Heart		enacting
	Sensing from the field			**Crystallizing** vision and intention
VoF	letting go	Open Will		letting come

Presencing
connecting to source

Who is my Self?
What is my Work?

Source: Presencing Institute, Otto Scharmer, www.presencing.com/permissions/

31 https://integralleadershipreview.com/10916-otto-scharmer-theory-u-leading-future-emerges/
32 https://interactioninstitute.org/theory-u-the-1st-proposition/
33 https://www.toolshero.com/leadership/theory-u-scharmer/
34 https://en.wikipedia.org/wiki/Theory_U

This change methodology consists of three main phases and seven capacities. Here's an illustration of each phase and its associated steps, along with questions to consider:

Sensing Phase (Left side of the U)

1. Downloading—Question: What is life calling me to do?
2. Seeing—Question: What do I see when I suspend judgment and open my mind?
3. Sensing—Question: What do I feel when I connect with my heart?

Presencing Phase (Bottom of the U)

4. Presencing—Questson: What is my deepest source of inspiration and will?

Realizing Phase (Right side of the U)

5. Crystallizing—Question: What is my vision and intention for the future?
6. Prototyping—Question: How can I integrate my head, heart, and hands to create a living example of my vision?
7. Performing—Question: How can I embody this new way of being and acting in the world?

The U-process involves moving through these phases, allowing you to let go of old patterns and embrace new ideas. As you journey down the left side of the U, you overcome resistance and open yourself to new perspectives. At the bottom, you connect with your deepest source of knowing. As you move up the right side, you bring forth new ideas and solutions into the world.

Now, let's apply this framework to the situation of an individual in their fifties. For employees in the late stage of their careers who are seeking to redefine their sense of work contributions, Theory U can be a powerful framework for personal transformation and rediscovery. Here's how they might apply each phase of Theory U:

Sensing Phase

1. **Downloading:** The employees should create time and mental space for reflection, free from distractions. They might ask themselves, "What is my work calling me to do at this stage of my career?"
2. **Seeing:** Individuals should observe their current work environments and roles with fresh eyes, suspending judgment. This might involve noting how their experience and skills are currently utilized and where they see opportunities for change.
3. **Sensing:** Older workers should connect with their hearts, exploring deeper motivations and values. They might reflect on what aspects of their work have been most fulfilling over the years.

Presencing Phase

Presencing: This is a crucial step, during which the employee connects with their deepest source of inspiration and will. Ask this question: "What is my highest future potential in the workplace, and how can I embody it now?"[35] This might involve visualizing the individual's ideal contribution or role.

Realizing Phase

1. **Crystallizing:** At this point, the employee develops a clear vision for a repurposed work contribution. They might ask, "What unique value can I bring to my organization or field at this stage of my career?"
2. **Prototyping:** Here, the employee experiments with new ways of working or contributing. This could involve proposing new projects, mentoring younger colleagues, or exploring different roles within the organization.
3. **Performing:** Finally, the employee fully embodies the new work identity. This might involve taking on new responsibilities, initi-

---

35 https://www.garrisoninstitute.org/the-future-of-leadership-will-be-more-feminine/

ating change within the organization, or even transitioning to a new role that better aligns with their crystallized vision.[36]

The example above illustrates how Theory U serves as both a framework and a how-to method. As mentioned above, the third aspect of the Theory U is a way of being, a kind of connection to the more authentic or the higher aspects of ourselves. This is particularly relevant for the mature employee: When people enter a company and get immersed into the corporate culture and the day-to-day work, they often start separating themselves (who they really are) from who they are at work. Gradually, this gap widens and they lose their sense of purpose (over a longer period of time). So, following the process of Theory U, entering the Presencing Phase, the individual begins to reconnect with their real self and develop an unfolding new sense of purpose. In this way, the individual's authentic self creates their future and shapes their career path.

As the participants go through these three phases, they will have to overcome obstacles. This happens through self-reflection and peer-to-peer discussion during the Catalyst Program:

Voice of Judgment

The first obstacle is the Voice of Judgment (VoJ)[37] —an internal voice that blocks the gate to an open mind, shuts down creativity and new possibilities, and represents our tendency to make quick judgments based on past experiences.[38]

To engage with Theory U, practitioners are encouraged to suspend their inner critics.[39] This involves resisting the habit to judge based on

---

36 https://confidentchangemanagement.com/book-reviews/psychology-neurology-philoso-phy/philosophy/theory-u-leading-from-the-future-as-it-emerges/
37 https://www.linkedin.com/pulse/core-principles-applications-from-essentials-theo-ry-u-prachi-mishra
38 https://www.dailygood.org/story/450/uncovering-the-blind-spot-of-leadership-c-otto-scharmer/
39 https://thesystemsthinker.com/leading-from-the-future-a-new-social-technology-for-our-times/

past experience and opening oneself to new perspectives and possibilities, observing situations with fresh eyes and an open mind. By suspending the Voice of Judgment, individuals can move down the left side of the U, which is about opening up and dealing with the resistance of thought, emotion, and will. This step is crucial for fostering creativity, innovation, and transformative change in personal and organizational contexts.

Voice of Cynicism

The second obstacle is the Voice of Cynicism (VoC),[40] which blocks the gate to an open heart. Overcoming the Voice of Cynicism involves redirecting attention from the object to its source, connecting with an open heart, and engaging in deep listening and dialogue. By addressing the Voice of Cynicism, individuals can move more effectively through the sensing phase of Theory U, allowing for a deeper connection with others and the emerging future.

Voice of Fear

The third obstacle is the Voice of Fear (VoF), which blocks the gate to an open will.[41] Overcoming the Voice of Fear requires one to let go of old identities and the need for control, surrender to the emerging future, and access one's authentic self and highest future potential. By confronting the Voice of Fear, individuals can move through the presencing phase of Theory U and connect with their deepest source of inspiration and will.

By following this process, older employees can tap into their wealth of experience and wisdom, overcome obstacles, find renewed purpose, and make meaningful contributions in their work lives. The Theory U approach allows them to break free of anchored patterns and see their

---

40 https://www.linkedin.com/pulse/core-principles-applications-from-essentials-theory-u-prachi-mishra/
41 https://en.wikipedia.org/wiki/Theory_U

professional landscape with fresh eyes, potentially leading to more fulfilling and impactful work in their later career stages.[42]

The participants in our Catalyst Program follow this seven-step framework to reflect on their value contribution in the context of their current job environments, as well as their professional and personal life experiences, and to align these insights with their current and future job requirements. The final step links personal insights to specific action. We call this the impact plan. Participants commit to specific actions intended to shift the way they embrace their current roles in order to drive change.

Here are some examples:

Thomas, a senior engineer in the radar development division of an aerospace company, who is also a sports enthusiast, used an analogy for shifting his focus in one area: "I want to add an away game to my daily work routine." He believes that, beyond his core engineering capabilities, he could leverage his expertise in supporting the recruitment of younger engineers, in addition to offering career development support for young people.

Martin, a substation engineer at an electric grid company, seeks ways to leverage his experience in risk evaluation and refinement of preventative maintenance. For him, this means taking a more vigilant and proactive approach, reaching across business functions instead of choosing to stay focused on his own area of responsibility.

Janine, the department head for technical procurement of a construction company, made a conscious choice to change the way she interacts with her team. Leaving the drumbeat of directive leadership, she models her own experience-based way of operating and decision-making. Leading by example, she empowers her team to make decisions based on their own experience and wisdom, for the benefit of the daily routine.

Although the area where people focus their attention varies, depending on their profession, career progression, and corporate circum-

---

42   https://edtechbooks.org/ldvoices/TheoryU_learning

stances—in every case, they share a feeling of being their own creators of success and fulfillment.

The individual who regains clarity on purpose, late-stage career goals, and work contributions will inevitably refocus personal energy and commitment. This often results in improved work processes and higher output. It not only improves personal engagement, motivation, and personal productivity, but also impacts the wider process improvement and quality enhancement.

The personal "impact plan," developed at the end of the Catalyst Program, summarizing the intended actions and impact, is shared with the respective manager and HR department to ensure alignment with the company's overarching objectives and strategy. Successful implementation of the plan (and aligned sustainable change) should be supported by careful follow-up and coaching interventions, where appropriate.

Processes

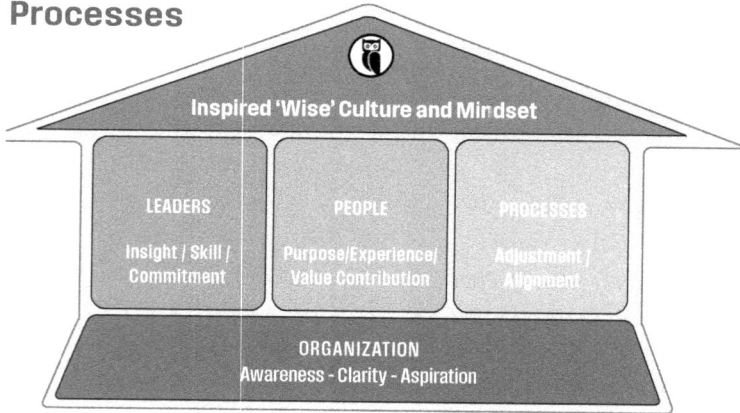

Inspired 'Wise' Culture and Mindset

LEADERS
Insight / Skill / Commitment

PEOPLE
Purpose/Experience/ Value Contribution

PROCESSES
Adjustment / Alignment

ORGANIZATION
Awareness - Clarity - Aspiration

© WiseForce Advisors

George, Senior VP of Controlling for a global IT service provider, participated in our Catalyst Program recently. He and his boss, Mike, who also participated in our training for enhanced leadership effectiveness of the 50+ workforce, were aligned on the way forward. George was supposed to continue in his current role supporting the business line's cloud transformation initiative for the next six months before he transitioned into the sustainability business line, helping clients improve the sustainability and resilience of their business models. When George reached out to his HR business partner to apply for an open position in the sustainability business line, he was immediately rejected: "Sorry, George, but it is our policy not to pursue applicants over the age of 55," they said.

Running a Wise Organization requires an adjustment and/or alignment of the organizational people processes to complete the triangulation between leaders, the 50+ employee base, and aligned processes. The people-process pillar is often overlooked, but is instrumental to achieving enhanced engagement of the aging workforce. In George's case, the outdated recruitment policy and a missing cultural adjustment that values mature talent led to a significant demotivation of an experienced contributor. Likewise, Mike, his boss, was equally disappointed and less likely to continue doing his part to shape the company into a Wise Organization.

Let's have a closer look at the people processes that are critically important to building a Wise Organization and learn how each element can be improved to leverage the potential of the 50+ workforce:
— core talent management
— skills and knowledge
— career development
— health and wellbeing

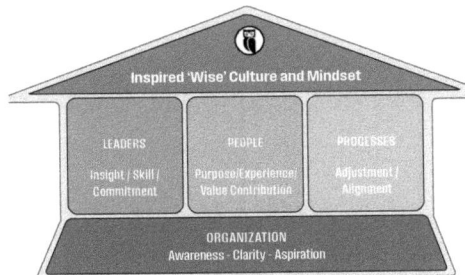

© WiseForce Advisors

Core Talent Management

The core talent management process includes attraction (employer brand), recruitment, and retention.

Attraction

To improve the employer brand for the future 50+ workforce, companies need to adapt their strategies to appeal to this experienced demographic. Here are specific examples of how to enhance your employer brand for the 50+ workforce:

Highlight experience and reliability: Emphasize the value of experience in your employer branding messages. Showcase how your company values the reliability and expertise that older workers bring to the table.[43] For instance, create testimonials or "day in the life" videos featuring successful 50+ employees in various roles within your organization.

Offer flexible work arrangements: Promote flexible work options that appeal to the 50+ demographic. This could include part-time positions, job sharing opportunities, remote work options, and seasonal or project-based roles. Highlight these flexible arrangements in your job postings and on your career website to attract experienced professionals seeking work-life balance.

Focus on continuous learning and development: Demonstrate your commitment to lifelong learning by:
- implementing mentorship programs where 50+ employees can share their knowledge with younger colleagues
- offering reverse mentoring opportunities where younger employees teach new technologies to older workers
- providing access to online courses and workshops for skill development
- hosting internal career fairs showcasing growth opportunities for all age groups

---

43 https://www.linkedin.com/pulse/experience-you-can-count-unlocking-power-50-work-force-zuknick-mba-w5pwe

Emphasize health and wellness benefits: Tailor your benefits package to address the needs of older workers through comprehensive health insurance plans, wellness programs focused on preventive care, employee assistance programs for mental health support, and ergonomic workplace assessments and accommodations. Highlight these benefits in your employer branding materials to show your commitment to supporting the well-being of all employees.

Showcase age diversity in marketing materials: Ensure your employer branding visuals represent age diversity by including images of 50+ employees in recruitment materials and on your career website, featuring success stories of older workers in company newsletters and social media posts, and creating video content showcasing intergenerational collaboration within your organization.

Develop a "returnship" program: Implement a "returnship" program specifically designed for experienced professionals re-entering the workforce after a career break. This initiative can be a powerful addition to your employer brand, demonstrating your commitment to tapping into the valuable skills of the 50+ workforce.

Highlight Corporate Social Responsibility (CSR) initiatives: Many older workers value giving back to the community. Showcase your company's CSR efforts and provide opportunities for 50+ employees to participate in meaningful volunteer work or mentorship programs within the community.

Showcase experience and expertise: Create an "Employee Spotlight" series focusing on the achievements and career journeys of 50+ workers.[44] This approach highlights the valuable contributions of older employees and demonstrates your company's appreciation for their expertise. Develop video content showcasing intergenerational collaboration and knowledge sharing within your organization.[45]

---

44 https://www.swoonstaffing.com/mastering-employer-branding-and-generational-diversity-for-a-thriving-workplace/

45 https://universumglobal.com/employer-branding/

Leverage social media and employee advocacy: Encourage older employees to become brand ambassadors on social media platforms. You can provide training on personal branding and guidelines for sharing company-related content.[46] Or recognize and appreciate employees who actively contribute to enhancing your employer brand through social media.[47]

Get involved in external representation: Engage experienced workers in representing the company at industry events and career fairs. This not only showcases the diversity of your workforce but also allows older employees to share their expertise and experiences with potential candidates.

Gather and act on feedback: Actively seek input from older employees to improve your employer brand. You can conduct surveys, focus groups, and one-on-one conversations to understand their perspectives. Then use these insights to refine your employer branding strategies and workplace policies.

Create inclusive content: Ensure your employer branding materials represent age diversity. Include images and stories of 50+ employees in recruitment materials and on your career website.[48] Also share employee testimonials and "day-in-the-life" videos that feature older workers, giving candidates a real feel for your inclusive workplace culture.

By implementing these strategies, you can create a strong employer brand that resonates with the 50+ workforce, tapping into a wealth of experience and addressing the unique needs and values of this segment.

46   https://www.joveo.com/blog/how-to-improve-employer-branding-best-practices-for-busi-
       ness-success/
47   https://cohorts.work/en/5-ways-to-engage-employees-in-employer-branding/
48   https://www.frontify.com/en/guide/employer-branding

Recruitment

Age-inclusive Hiring Processes

An age-inclusive hiring process aims to eliminate bias and create equal opportunities for candidates of all ages. Here are nine detailed examples:

1. **Age-neutral job descriptions:** Job postings focus on skills and competencies rather than years of experience.[49] They avoid age-specific terms like "digital native" or "recent graduate." For example, instead of "Seeking energetic, young professional with two to three years of experience," use "Seeking motivated individual with strong problem-solving skills and relevant experience in project management."

2. **Diverse recruitment channels:** Employers use a mix of platforms to reach candidates of all ages.[50] This includes online job boards and social media, print media and local newspapers, community organizations and job centers, professional associations, and employee referrals.

3. **Blind recruitment techniques:** Initial screening removes age-related information from resumes. For instance, redacting graduation dates and birth years, and focusing on skills and achievements rather than chronological work history.

4. **Structured interviews:** Interviews use consistent questions for all candidates, focusing on skills and competencies. For example, "Describe a situation where you successfully led a team through a challenging project." Or, "How do you stay up to date with industry trends and new technologies?"

5. **Diverse interview panels:** Panels include interviewers from various age groups to provide different perspectives. For example, a

---

49 https://www.linkedin.com/pulse/guide-age-inclusive-recruitment-unlocking-potential-ian-wilkinson-0cyge and https://www.findmyprofession.com/career-advice/combat-ageism-in-hiring/

50 https://interviewvector.com/blogs/inclusive-hiring/ and https://www.linkedin.com/pulse/creating-age-inclusive-recruitment-strategy-practical-steps-success-bir4e

panel might consist of a Gen X manager, a Millennial team lead, and a Baby Boomer executive.

6. **Age bias training:** Providing training to hiring managers and recruiters to recognize and combat age-related biases might include workshops on the value of age diversity, case studies demonstrating the impact of age-inclusive teams, and unconscious bias training specific to age stereotypes.

7. **Inclusive company culture promotion:** Showcase age diversity in marketing materials and during the recruitment process. For instance, you could feature employees of various ages in company videos and brochures and highlight multigenerational teams in job advertisements.

8. **Skills-based assessments:** Use practical tests or simulations to evaluate candidates' abilities, regardless of age. Examples include coding challenges for software developers, writing/visual samples for content creators, or role-playing exercises for customer service positions.

By implementing these practices, organizations can create an age-inclusive hiring process that values the talent and contributions from all generations.

Flexible Work Arrangements

Consider offering options that appeal to different age groups, such as part-time and job-sharing positions[51] [52], remote work opportunities, flexible hours, and job-protected time off. Task flexibility is an innovative approach for older workers that involves redesigning jobs to support changing physical and intellectual capacities[53]. For example, you might remove physically demanding tasks, provide support from col-

51 https://zenohealthgroup.com/7-essential-strategies-to-activate-an-ageing-workforce/
52 https://www.linkedin.com/pulse/strategic-solutions-challenges-posed-aging-workforce
53 https://www.vercida.com/uk/articles/older-workers-flexible-working-arrangements

leagues for challenging tasks, or move employees to roles more suited to their current abilities.

Other flexible work arrangements include **annualized hours**, where working time for some 50+ workers is calculated on an annual rather than weekly basis,[54] **term-time working**, through which some of your older workers have agreements allowing them to work only during school terms, and job sharing, which allows two part-time employees to share the responsibilities of one full-time position.

These types of innovative work arrangements accommodate the lifestyle needs and health considerations of older workers, while allowing organizations to retain valuable experience and skills.

Retention

Opportunities to increase employee retention include:

Redesigning roles: Rethinking job roles can maximize the contributions of older workers. You might create positions that leverage the experience and wisdom of seasoned employees,[55] redesign tasks to accommodate changing physical capabilities,[56] offer project-based work or consulting roles for those seeking reduced hours, or use AI and automation to reduce mundane tasks, allowing older workers to focus on higher-value activities.[57]

Implementing mentorship programs: Establish cross-generational mentorship initiatives that showcase the value of experienced workers. Some companies create reverse mentoring opportunities, through which younger employees teach new technologies to older workers. Others implement programs that facilitate knowledge transfer between generations, benefiting both newer and more experienced employees.

---

54 https://www.thephoenixgroup.com/media/ch0eta1h/flexible-after-fifty-report.pdf
55 https://acuityinternational.com/blog/aging-workforce/
56 https://www.weforum.org/agenda/2023/05/how-workplaces-can-adapt-to-an-ageing-workforce/
57 https://humanforce.com/gb/blog/the-ageing-workforce-how-to-leverage-the-experiences-of-older-workers-to-increase-employee-engagement/

Professional training: Research indicates that participating in professional training and development correlates with a lower risk of leaving current employment. Specifically, continuous learning opportunities are associated with increased intention to stay in a current job, decreased intention to leave a current job, and reduced employee turnover intention.

Skills and Knowledge

Skill and knowledge management plays a key role in managing your organization wisely. But evidence shows that organizations could do much better: According to a 2024 OECD study on career path and engagement of mature workers, mature workers are less likely to participate in training compared to their younger counterparts. With more than 40 percent participation, mature workers (55+) in the US and New Zealand receive the most training, far outperforming the average of 25 percent.[58]

younger workers

Share of adults who participated in formal or non-formal job-related training over the previous 12 months

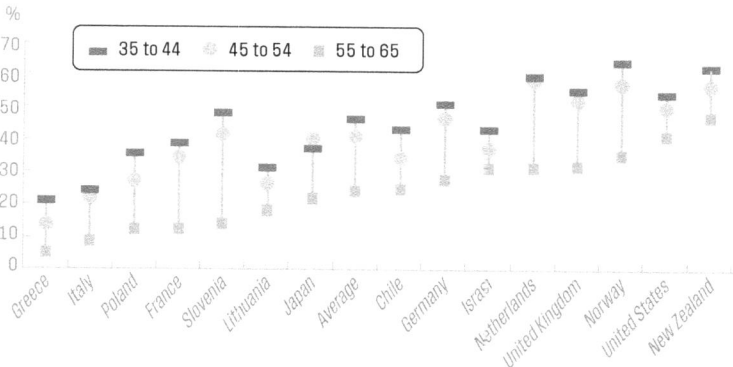

Source: https://www.oecd.org/content/dam/oecd/en/topics/policy-issues/ageing-and-employment/Career-Paths-and-Engagement-of-Mature-Workers.pdf

---

58 https://www.oecd.org/content/dam/oecd/en/topics/policy-issues/ageing-and-employment/Career-Paths-and-Engagement-of-Mature-Workers.pdf

Let's have a closer look at individual skills development and knowledge transfer of valuable institutional knowledge, as well as functional and market knowledge.

Engagement and Motivation

Providing ongoing learning opportunities helps keep older workers engaged and motivated in their roles. Continuous learning is a key factor in retaining older employees, as it helps them stay current and feel valued. By offering training programs and workshops tailored to their specific needs, organizations can keep mature workers intellectually stimulated and committed to their work. Furthermore, continuous learning is also an important prerequisite for leveraging one's own experience effectively.

Skill Development and Relevance

Continuous learning is absolutely critical for older workers to stay employable—particularly as the workplace evolves rapidly, and staying competitive and valuable to their organizations is crucial. Continuous learning also plays a vital role in retaining older workers and leveraging their potential for innovation, growth, and productivity. Here's how:

- **Bridging generational gaps:** Continuous learning programs can help bridge knowledge gaps between generations. When older and younger workers participate in training together, it fosters knowledge sharing and collaboration. This can lead to a more cohesive and productive multigenerational workforce.

- **Addressing skills gaps:** Lifelong learning is crucial for addressing skills gaps that may develop over time. Recent research showed that adults aged 55 and over are at the highest risk of being left behind when it comes to formal training.[59] By providing targeted learning opportunities, employers can ensure that older workers' skills remain relevant and valuable to the organization.

---

59 https://www.reedtalentsolutions.com/articles/how-employers-can-address-skills-gaps-in-older-workers

- **Enhancing confidence and job satisfaction:** Continuous learning can boost older workers' confidence in their abilities, particularly when it comes to new technologies or processes. This increased confidence often translates to higher job satisfaction and productivity—and a satisfying career advancement.

Succession Planning and Knowledge Preservation

Creating a supportive culture that values knowledge sharing is fundamental. This can be achieved through open communication about the importance of preserving institutional knowledge, encouraging collaborative projects, and recognizing contributions from senior employees.[60] In addition, investing in upskilling and reskilling programs is vital for older employees to adapt to technological changes. It can also be seen as a way to preserve knowledge. Organizations should create inclusive learning environments that encourage knowledge sharing between generations through mutual mentoring programs. This approach not only benefits individual employees but also strengthens the overall skill set of the organization.

Involving all employees in the succession planning process fosters a culture of shared responsibility for knowledge preservation. Engaging older workers in discussions about their career aspirations and legacy can lead to more effective transition strategies.[61]

Mentorship and Knowledge Transfer Programs

Emphasizing opportunities for cross-generational learning could include mentoring or reverse mentoring programs that pair younger and older employees, as well as collaborative projects that leverage diverse experiences

---

60 https://edz.bib.uni-mannheim.de/www-edz/pdf/ef/98/ef9865en.pdf
61 https://www.syndeohro.com/post/whats-a-succession-plan-for-an-aging-workforce and
    https://hortoninternational.com/planning-ahead-for-an-aging-workforce/

Several companies have implemented successful knowledge transfer programs for older workers, ensuring their valuable expertise is preserved within the organization. Here are some exemplary initiatives:

BNL BNP Paribas: Cross-Generational Coaching Program

BNL BNP Paribas launched an internal cross-generational coaching program across its offices in Italy in 2022.[62] This initiative includes:

- a Train-the-Trainer program for employees aged 45 and above
- training in lesson organization, class management, and participant engagement
- experts delivering three-hour webinars to share their knowledge
- more than 180 hours of courses delivered since 2022
- an expanded Expert Learning Community of 69 members

The program has proven cost-effective in disseminating knowledge and fostering a culture that values older workers' talents.

BAE Systems: Knowledge Transfer Groups

BAE Systems, a multinational defense and aerospace company, has implemented a proactive approach to knowledge transfer:[63]

- formation of knowledge-transfer groups when an employee with deep institutional knowledge plans to retire
- groups consist of about half a dozen people of varying ages working in the same area
- regular meetings over months for advice exchange and gradual task handoff
- quantified savings of $120,000 to $180,000 per project on average

62 https://www.oecd.org/content/dam/oecd/en/topics/policy-issues/ageing-and-employment/Facilitating-knowledge-transfer-between-generations.pdf/_jcr_content/renditions/original./Facilitating-knowledge-transfer-between-generations.pdf

63 https://www.linkedin.com/pulse/how-knowledge-transfer-effectively-across-generations-ryan-jenkins

Mentorship and Job Shadowing Programs

Many organizations have found success with structured mentorship and job shadowing initiatives.[64] In these programs, experienced employees train new hires on machine operation, troubleshooting, and safety protocols in manufacturing plants—while senior software developers mentor new hires on coding best practices, software architecture, and testing methodologies, for example. These formal mentorship opportunities may also come with recognition and rewards for mentors. Intergenerational job shadowing provides on-the-job transfer of tacit knowledge.

Knowledge Sharing Platforms and Tools

Increasingly, companies are leveraging technology to facilitate knowledge transfer.[65] These efforts can look like:

- implementation of forums, wikis, or knowledge databases for sharing insights and best practices
- creation of infographics by veteran employees to distill expertise
- video recordings and screencasts of experienced workers demonstrating effective techniques
- internal company podcasts featuring interviews with experienced employees

Flexible Roles for Knowledge Advisors

Some organizations are creating specialized positions for knowledge transfer. We are seeing "knowledge advisor" or "internal consultant" roles for employees nearing retirement. These positions focus on sharing expertise, offering guidance, and conducting training sessions, resulting in reduced pressure for regular tasks while maximizing knowledge transfer.

---

64 https://eguides.osha.europa.eu/all-ages/knowledge-transfer-training-and-life-long-learning
65 https://projectjumpstarttraining.org/uncategorized/5-strategies-to-encourage-knowledge-sharing-among-older-employees/ and https://www.rewo.io/transfer-knowledge-next-generation-workers/

These examples demonstrate how companies can harness the expertise of older workers, ensuring valuable knowledge is retained and transferred to younger generations within the organization.

Career Development

According to the 2024 OECD study on the career paths and engagement of mature workers, employers have few policies in place to support career development and planning.

Employers have few policies in place to support career development and planning
Share of employers that have fully, somewhat or not at all implemented a specific policy for mature workers (>55 years)

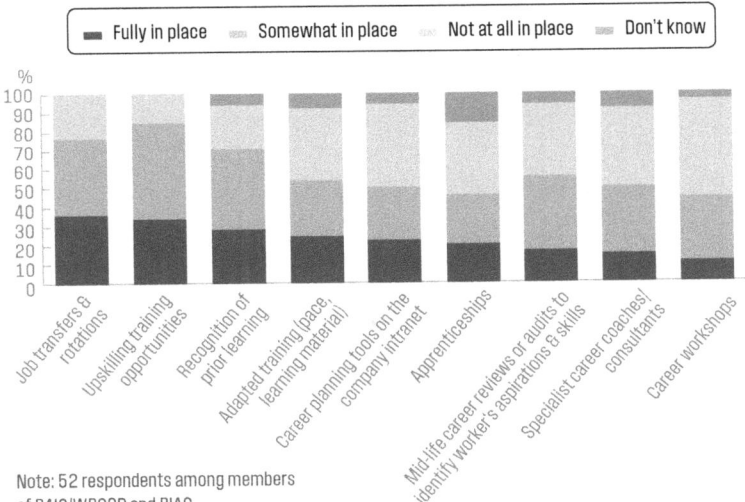

Note: 52 respondents among members of B4IG/WBCSD and BIAC.

Source: 2024 OECD/B4IG/WBCSD Multigenerational workforce survey. https://www.oecd.org/content/dam/oecd/en/topics/policy-issues/ageing-and-employment/Career-Paths-and-Engagement-

When we look at responses to the "mid-life career review or audits to identify worker's aspirations and skills," only 15 percent of companies report having policies in place, whereas 80 percent have such policies only somewhat or not at all in place.

If an organization does not have a policy and process for the mid-life career review, the responsibility falls to the individual manager and employee to address the issue. This lack of structure and commitment puts a huge strain on late-stage career development, and it will affect the employee's productivity and wellbeing.

Confronted with this situation, the majority of the people leaders in an organization will refer to conversations they have with their subordinates. As explained in Chapter 5, people leaders may touch on this conversation in the annual performance review (wrong occasion!) or find another opportunity to discuss the topic, but they may not have the understanding to handle the situation wisely.

Earlier in this chapter, I stressed the importance of individual reflection and creating a new sense of purpose and work contribution through the Catalyst Program, as a structured process to support the career development of the mature worker.

In addition to this program, we are seeing some other successful interventions emerging:[66]

Schneider Electric, a French conglomerate, launched an initiative to help its 50+ employees "design the last miles of their careers." At the core of this program are career workshops, which prepare both experienced workers and their managers to engage in meaningful career conversations at least once a year.

Avia, one of the UK's leading insurance, wealth, and retirement businesses, runs a structured "mid-life review" process for its 45+ employees. The group seminar aims to provide information and opportunities to mid-career employees by holistically assessing their skills, financial security, wellbeing, and future retirement planning. Considering multiple facets of work life, these reviews serve as an initial step in ensuring that work at older ages remains fulfilling and sustainable. They act as a trigger to take stock and start reflecting on shifting work needs well before the choices become limited and change is no longer feasible.

66 https://www.oecd.org/content/dam/oecd/en/topics/policy-issues/ageing-and-employment/Career-Paths-and-Engagement-of-Mature-Workers.pdf

Barclays, the British universal bank, successfully launched an apprenticeship for people over the age of 50, as a vehicle to re-skill and stay employed.

The US publisher **Houghton Mifflin Harcourt** runs a job rotation program for experienced employees, resulting in a more engaged and experienced internal leadership pipeline.

Robert Bosch, the German engineering and technology company, is known for its Senior Experts Program, established in 1999 through Bosch Management Support GmbH (BMS).[67] This program allows retired Bosch employees to register as senior experts and share their knowledge with younger colleagues. Key features of this program include:

— over 2,400 senior experts worldwide
— more than 50,000 years of combined professional experience
— experts work on various projects, including development, production, and mentoring
— branches in multiple countries, including Brazil, India, and China

Allianz, the international financial services provider headquartered in Munich, Germany, focuses its efforts for age inclusion through Allianz Eng*AGE*, an employee network for age inclusion with 10 local networks in place. Through Allianz Eng*AGE*, employees are invited to proactively contribute to a company culture where the knowledge of all generations is called upon and people can continue to thrive throughout the different stages of their lives. Allianz Eng*AGE* focuses on supporting the company's culture of lifelong learning, supporting knowledge transfer between generations, opening a dialogue on what it means to manage and work in age-diverse teams, as well as bringing different experiences and mindsets into the organization.[68]

ALTANA, the German chemical company, introduced a program in 2023 called the Wise Peers Program. This effort represents the

---

67   https://www.bosch.com/stories/senior-experts-at-bosch/
68   https://www.allianz.com/en/about-us/strategy-values/diversity/allianz_engage.html

firm's initial initiative to champion diversity, equality, and inclusion within ALTANA. This program is specifically tailored for individuals who have been with the company for more than 20 years. The program commenced with an inaugural pilot group at the beginning of 2024. It focuses on topics such as knowledge transfer, lifelong learning, and appreciation.[69]

Japanese conglomerate **Mitsubishi Corporation** created a Career Design Center to provide comprehensive support for the firm's senior employees aged 60 and over.[70] The center offers three main benefits:

1. individualized career planning consultation based on each employee's personal situation and values
2. provision of various information and training programs for employees who wish to continue their careers outside the company
3. collection of recruitment and job matching information

The Career Design Center serves multiple functions. It supports the Re-Employment Course System, which extends the careers of employees aged 60 and over. It offers private counseling for seniors, assisting with external career changes. And it helps address the diverse awareness and opinions regarding working beyond the age of 60.

This initiative is part of Mitsubishi Corporation's broader efforts to promote diversity and support employees at various stages of their careers.

The Japanese gas company, **Tokyo Gas,** launched a comprehensive program called Grand Career System designed to support and retain employees over 50 years old. The system offers several benefits for the company's aging workforce:[71]

1. Career development support: The program provides structured assistance to help older employees plan and advance their careers.

69 https://www.altana.com/press-news/publications/corporate-report-2023/people.html
70 https://mitsubishicorp.disclosure.site/en/themes/120/
71 https://www.bain.com/insights/better-with-age-the-rising-importance-of-older-workers/

2. Customized training: Employees receive tailored training to enhance their skills and keep them relevant in the workforce.

3. One-on-one mentoring: Personalized guidance is offered to address individual career needs and challenges.

4. Job matching: The system helps match older employees with suitable positions within the company or its subsidiaries.

5. High retention rate: As a result of these initiatives, more than 90 percent of Tokyo Gas workers facing mandatory retirement were rehired by the company or its subsidiaries.[72]

The list of innovative career development tools that can support older workers' career development is long and varied. Here are a few more ideas to try:

— Create interactive internal career pages for exploring new opportunities.
— Offer career guidance through online platforms and informal meetups.
— Conduct regular career conversations with managers or career coaches.
— Implement job shadowing and rotation programs to help older workers discover new roles within the organization.
— Conduct skills assessments: Evaluate the skills, knowledge, and expertise of experienced workers to identify areas where their talents can be utilized.[73]
— Create tailored roles: Develop positions that capitalize on the unique strengths and experiences of mid-career professionals, allowing them to contribute their expertise effectively.[74]

72 https://www.growthspace.com/post/investing-in-older-workers
73 https://disprz.ai/blog/how-to-identify-knowledge-and-skill-gaps
74 https://www.generation.org/news/recognizing-and-leveraging-the-expertise-of-midca-reer-professionals/

- Encourage cross-functional projects: Involve experienced workers in initiatives that span multiple departments, allowing them to apply their broad knowledge base.[75]
- Develop "edge cases": Identify specific scenarios where redesigning employee journeys can add the most value for experienced workers.[76]
- Focus on strengths and interests: Align roles and responsibilities with the strengths and passions of experienced workers to increase engagement and productivity.[77]
- Create role offshoots: Develop side projects or additional responsibilities that allow experienced workers to expand their expertise within their current positions.[78]
- Leverage partnerships: Collaborate with community organizations and networks to identify experienced talent and create opportunities for their involvement.[79]

As a side note, flexible work arrangements and lifelong learning initiatives have an impact on career development as well. As these topics have been addressed above, I did not further outline them in this chapter.

By implementing the solutions above, companies can effectively support the career development of their older employees, leading to increased engagement, productivity, and retention of valuable experience and knowledge.

75 https://www.mckinsey.com/capabilities/people-and-organizational-performance/our-insights/this-time-its-personal-shaping-the-new-possible-through-employee-experience
76 https://www.mckinsey.com/capabilities/people-and-organizational-performance/our-insights/this-time-its-personal-shaping-the-new-possible-through-employee-experience
77 https://www.adp.com/spark/articles/2024/03/rethinking-career-transitions-how-giving-employees-leverage-can-be-a-winwin.aspx
78 https://www.adp.com/spark/articles/2024/03/rethinking-career-transitions-how-giving-employees-leverage-can-be-a-winwin.aspx
79 https://hr.wisc.edu/equity-inclusion-and-employee-well-being/resources/leveraging-the-employee-experience/

Health and Wellbeing

Bill has been the production line leader in a global automotive supply company for many years. At some point, he was asked what he considered to be his biggest responsibility in the metal forming business. His answer was prompt and with conviction: "To keep my people safe and healthy."

The evolution of health and safety in manufacturing companies has been a long and transformative journey, spanning over two centuries. This progression has been marked by significant events, technological advances, and changing societal attitudes.

In the 18th and 19th centuries, workers often faced dangerous conditions with little protection. Early forms of personal protection developed in the late 19th and early 20th centuries with the appointment of industry inspectors. Later, the creation of the Occupational Safety and Health Administration (OSHA) in the US in 1970 marked a turning point, establishing federal oversight for workplace safety.[80] Likewise, the establishment of the European Agency for Safety and Health at Work (EU-OSHA) in 1996 aimed to make workplaces safer, healthier, and more productive by providing relevant technical, scientific, and economic information on occupational safety and health.[81] The current framework (2022-2027) serves as a foundation for EU-OSHA's multi-annual strategic program focusing on key priority areas to improve workplace safety across Europe.[82]

The advent of the Internet and digital technologies has transformed health and safety management, bringing about a shift from reactive to proactive approaches using predictive analytics, IoT, and mobile technologies. Companies are also implementing real-time monitoring and response systems for health and safety risks. Increasingly, we're seeing the integration of environment, health, and safety

---

80 https://www.oranaskillscentre.com/post/the-evolution-of-workplace-health-and-safety-a-global-perspective
81 https://www.baua.de/EN/About-BAuA/Tasks/Cooperations/EU-OSHA
82 https://www.baua.de/EN/About-BAuA/Tasks/Cooperations/EU-OSHA

(EHS) management into broader business operations and strategic decision-making.[83]

Today, health and safety in companies are characterized by a holistic approach that considers not just physical safety but mental health and wellbeing, too.[84] Safety management is integrated with enterprise systems and business intelligence,[85] and the use of advanced management tools with embedded EHS functionality is on the rise.[86] More and more, leaders seem to be focusing on creating a safety culture, in which all employees are empowered to take action against unsafe conditions.[87]

The future of health and safety is likely to involve an even greater emphasis on mental health and stress management in the workplace,[88] as well as continued integration of technology, including AI and machine learning, for predictive safety measures. We also can expect to see an increased focus on sustainability and environmental impact alongside traditional safety concerns. This evolution reflects a growing recognition that employee safety and wellbeing are not just ethical imperatives but key factors in operational efficiency, productivity, and overall business success.

Workplace health and safety concern the entire organization, but generational shifts have shaped the approach, as well as the expectations of employers, so it is worth taking a closer look.

83 https://www.l2l.com/blog/ehs-manufacturing
84 https://www.oranaskillscentre.com/post/the-evolution-of-workplace-health-and-safety-a-global-perspective
85 https://www.l2l.com/blog/ehs-manufacturing
86 https://www.l2l.com/blog/ehs-manufacturing
87 https://www.domtar.com/manufacturing-safety-at-domtar/
88 https://www.oranaskillscentre.com/post/the-evolution-of-workplace-health-and-safety-a-global-perspective

Generational Shifts in Workplace Health and Safety Expectations

Each generation brings unique perspectives, values, and expectations to the workplace, influenced by the societal, economic, and technological conditions in which they were raised. These generational differences shape their approach to workplace health and safety (WHS), as well as their expectations of employers. Here is a summary, based on a 2024 post by the Orana Skills Centre:[89]

Baby Boomers (1946–1964): The Foundational Generation

Key Influences:

– post-World War II industrial growth

– introduction of basic labor laws and workplace safety regulations

Expectations:

– compliance-focused safety: emphasize adherence to safety rules and regulations

– hierarchical structures: expect clear chains of command and defined responsibilities for safety

– physical safety over psychosocial safety: focus on preventing accidents and injuries, rather than addressing mental health or work-life balance

– experience-driven decision-making: value practical experience and workplace traditions in shaping WHS policies

Challenges:

– hesitation to adopt new technologies like wearables or AI-driven safety tools

– possibility of perceiving newer approaches to WHS (e.g., psychosocial safety) as less critical, compared to traditional physical safety measures

---

89 https://www.oranaskillscentre.com/post/the-evolution-of-workplace-health-and-safety-a-global-perspective

Generation X (1965-1980): The Pragmatic Innovators

Key Influences:

- economic downturns in the 1970s and 1930s
- introduction of risk management and leadership-driven safety programs

Expectations:

- risk management approach: prefer systematic, proactive approaches to identifying and mitigating risks
- flexibility and innovation: open to implementing new safety technologies and systems that improve efficiency and outcomes
- leadership accountability: expect leadership to take active roles in fostering a safety culture
- balanced focus: acknowledge both physical and psychosocial safety concerns

Challenges:

- Balancing traditional WHS methods with the need to adapt to modern safety technologies and mental health awareness

Millennials (1981-1996): The Tech-Savvy Collaborators

Key Influences:

- digital revolution and the rise of social media
- increased focus on employee wellbeing and workplace diversity

Expectations:

- data-driven WHS: value the integration of technology (e.g., apps, wearables, AI) for real-time safety monitoring and reporting
- work-life balance: expect employers to prioritize mental health, flexible working conditions, and wellness initiatives
- collaborative culture: favor a participatory approach to WHS, with workers involved in decision-making and feedback loops
- transparency: demand open communication about safety initiatives, risks, and outcomes

Challenges:
- possibility of higher turnover rates making it difficult to sustain long-term safety training and awareness
- expectation of rapid adoption of safety technologies, which may be challenging for slower-moving industries

Gen Z (1997-2012): The Digital Natives

Key Influences:
- grew up with smartphones, social media, and instant access to information
- heightened awareness of social and environmental issues

Expectations:
- tech-first safety: expect cutting-edge safety technologies, including automation, AI, and immersive training (e.g., VR simulations)
- inclusive WHS policies: strong emphasis on diversity, equity, and inclusion in safety initiatives, including gender-specific PPE
- mental health as a priority: view mental health and psychosocial risks as critical WHS components
- sustainability in WHS: align safety practices with environmental sustainability and corporate social responsibility goals

Challenges:
- relatively short attention spans, potentially requiring innovative, engaging approaches to WHS training
- strong preference for flexible work arrangements and modern workplace designs, possibly posing a challenge for traditional industries

Generation Alpha (2013-2025): The Upcoming Generation

Predicted Influences:
- immersion in AI, automation, and advanced technologies from a young age

- raised with heightened awareness of climate change, global health crises, and social justice movements

Predicted Expectations:

- hyper-connected safety systems: will expect WHS systems to integrate seamlessly with their personal devices and workplace technologies
- gamified training: will demand engaging, gamified safety training experiences that use AR and VR
- customizable work environments: will expect workplaces to adapt to individual preferences, including ergonomic workspaces and personalized safety measures
- environmental and social integration: will align WHS practices with broader sustainability and ethical goals
- continuous feedback loops: will desire frequent, real-time updates on WHS metrics and initiatives, with a focus on transparency and inclusivity

Challenges:

- potential need for industries to adopt more adaptive, tech-driven solutions to meet this generation's expectations
- Balancing hyper-personalization with the scalability of WHS systems

The aging workforce in the context of this book encompasses the Baby Boomers, who prioritize physical safety over psychosocial safety, and who focus on preventing accidents and injuries rather than addressing mental health or work-life balance, as well as the early wave of Generation X, who expect leadership to take active roles in fostering a safety culture, acknowledging both physical and psychosocial safety concerns. With more employees over the age of 50 than ever before working in organizations, it is worth reconsidering and potentially adjusting existing policies and measures.

How does physical safety play out in a hazardous production environment, when workers are close to 70 years old? And with the advent of new technologies embedded in the workplace, how could psychosocial safety (encompassing mental, social, and emotional aspects) be challenged, leading to an unhealthy state of mind that could in turn jeopardize physical safety or product quality, or lead to increased sick leave?

When we talk about health and wellbeing in the context of an aging workforce, taking action is mandatory. Every organization needs to recognize the quiet shifts in perception, decision-making, and behavior that come with age.

Industry-specific focus

Wise Management health and wellbeing processes may need to be tailored to specific industries to maximize the desired impact. Here are some suggestions:

Manufacturing and Labor-Intensive Industries
- Focus on ergonomic workplace design to accommodate the physical limitations of older workers.
- Implement job rotation and task variation to reduce physical strain.
- Provide targeted training on new technologies and automation systems.

Healthcare and Social Services
- Leverage older workers' experience in patient care and communication.
- Implement flexible scheduling to accommodate the health needs of aging staff.
- Develop mentorship programs to transfer specialized medical knowledge.

Retail and Customer Service
- Utilize older workers' communication skills and patience in customer-facing roles.
- Offer part-time and flexible work arrangements.

- Provide training on new point-of-sale technologies and digital customer service tools.

Technology and IT
- Implement reverse mentoring programs, through which younger employees teach older workers about new technologies.
- Offer continuous learning opportunities to keep skills updated.
- Create mixed-age teams to combine experience with fresh perspectives.

Finance and Professional Services
- Leverage older workers' deep industry knowledge and client relationships.
- Implement knowledge management systems to capture expertise.
- Offer phased retirement options to retain valuable experience.

Education
- Utilize experienced educators as mentors for new teachers.
- Implement team-teaching approaches that pair older and younger educators.
- Provide training on new educational technologies and teaching methods.

Construction and Trades
- Focus on safety measures and ergonomic tools for older workers.
- Implement apprenticeship programs, in which older workers train newcomers.
- Offer roles that transition from physical labor to supervisory or planning positions.

Creative Industries
- Leverage older workers' expertise in project management and client relations.

- Implement cross-generational creative teams.
- Provide training on new digital tools and platforms.

In addition to these suggestions, consider these additional options, which apply across industries:

1. Tailor flexible work arrangements to industry-specific needs and constraints.
2. Develop industry-specific health and wellness programs.
3. Create knowledge transfer initiatives that address unique industry challenges.
4. Implement succession planning strategies that consider industry-specific skill requirements.
5. Adapt recruitment and retention strategies to address industry-specific talent shortages.

These lists of ideas are by no means exhaustive; the possibilities are limitless once you begin to get creative.

By tailoring Wise Management health and wellbeing strategies to the specific needs and characteristics of each industry, organizations can leverage the strengths of their aging workforce while addressing industry-specific challenges.

Culture and Mindset

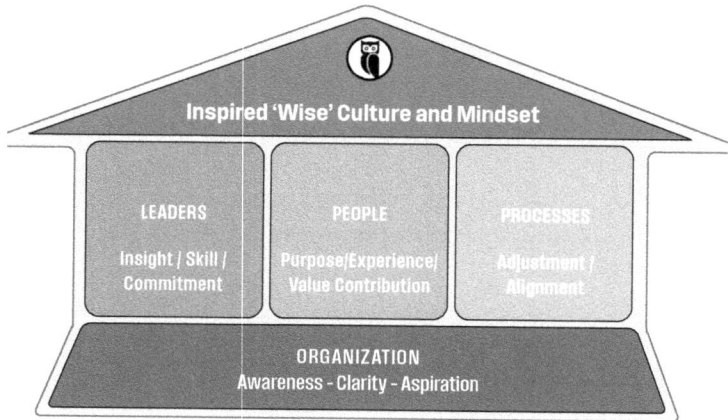

Inspired 'Wise' Culture and Mindset

LEADERS	PEOPLE	PROCESSES
Insight / Skill / Commitment	Purpose/Experience/ Value Contribution	Adjustment / Alignment

ORGANIZATION
Awareness - Clarity - Aspiration

© WiseForce Advisors

Each of the initiatives described in this chapter will contribute to shaping an inspired, Wise culture and mindset. But let's bring the topic of culture and mindset into a larger business context.

By now, you understand that almost all organizations are experiencing a dramatic shift in age distribution, which has a huge impact on how to lead the organization to achieve key business objectives with an aging workforce.

Likewise, the developing labor shortage as a consequence of the Baby Boomer generation retiring puts an additional burden on corporate performance. A Wise Organization, as outlined earlier in this book, leverages the collective experience of the entire employee base to sharpen its competitive edge and execute on strategic business priorities. This approach aligns with the needs of the aging worker and facilitates intergenerational communication and teamwork to leverage the unique strengths of each age group for the benefit of the organization and the wellbeing of older individuals.

L'Oréal for All Generations

L'Oréal Groupe, the French multinational personal care company, underpins its mindset and intergenerational culture with its "For All Generations" program.[90] It is remarkable how L'Oreal positions the program's purpose—as an answer to the three major global challenges of demographic, technological, and ecological changes. All three of these challenges pose opportunities and threats. The company has decided to embrace a people-centric mindset to counter the challenges ahead. L'Oréal wants to be the most inclusive, inspiring, and innovative company—one in which everyone has a place, regardless of age and experience, in order to thrive in the future. And the concept of employability throughout each person's career needs to stay top of mind.

L'Oréal launched "For All Generations" in France in 2022 and is now rolling the program out in Europe, China, and the US. Actions include advertising in major newspapers—what a remarkable brand statement! And this differentiating mindset goes even further with the alumni network Generations L'Oreal Association, for retired employees who want to stay connected and engaged with the firm.

L'Oréal is a great example of how to make intergenerationality and employability throughout one's career a real lever for growth and innovation.

Shaping a Wise Organization in response to shifting age demographics represents a uniquely strategic and proactive approach, compared to the more reactive methods of age management or age diversity management. You will be able to turn an aging workforce into a competitive advantage only with a Wise approach. Leadership plays a crucial role in fostering a wise culture by setting the tone, implementing policies, and modeling inclusive behaviors. Here are key ways leadership can influence age inclusivity:

---

90   https://www.loreal.com/en/germany/pages/commitments/seniors-de/

Set the vision and culture: Leaders act as architects of organizational culture, shaping the ethos that permeates throughout the company. By prioritizing a Wise Organization in their vision, leaders establish a foundation for an inclusive workplace where employees of all ages feel valued and respected.

Lead by example: Leaders of a Wise Organization demonstrate empathy, openness, and a commitment to diversity across all age groups. When leaders actively engage with employees from different age demographics and listen to their concerns, it sends a powerful message that age inclusivity is a top priority.

Promote accountability: Leaders must hold themselves and others accountable for fostering a Wise Organization. This involves addressing age-related biases and discriminatory behavior promptly and decisively, without exceptions.

Encourage diverse perspectives: Wise leaders actively seek out diverse perspectives and experiences across age groups. By creating an environment where people of all ages feel comfortable expressing their opinions, leaders can tap into the collective wisdom and innovation potential of a multi-generational workforce.

Invest in training and education: Providing unconscious bias training that specifically addresses age-related biases can help raise awareness and equip leaders with tools to promote the potential of all ages within their teams. Higher levels of awareness will further shape a Wise culture.

Create a culture of belonging: Ultimately, Wise leaders strive to create a culture in which employees of all ages feel valued and appreciated, regardless of their differences. This sense of belonging can lead to increased engagement, productivity, and retention across all age groups.

Creating a Future-Ready Council

To further shape the culture and mindset, create a future-ready council—a group of employees that focuses on preparing the organization for upcoming challenges and opportunities. This is another way of building a Wise Organization. The primary tasks of a future-ready council include:

1. fostering collaborative leadership by empowering stakeholders at all levels to innovate and contribute to the organization's vision of a Wise Organization[91]

2. supporting the implementation of strategic plans that align with the organization's forward-thinking vision, incorporating input from various stakeholders[92]

3. cultivating a culture of adaptability, agility, and continuous learning

4. promoting new approaches to help the workforce better understand how a Wise Organization benefits everybody

5. focusing on long-term sustainability and sharing best practices for continuous improvement[93]

6. modernizing learning strategies to develop a workforce that's always learning and adapting to new skill requirements[94]

7. fostering an inclusive culture that supports diversity and addresses evolving social and cultural priorities

8. supporting the development of a purpose-led employer brand to attract and retain talent from all age groups

As you apply these Wise Management principles in each of the five areas as outlined in this chapter, you will build a Wise Organization step-by-step. Continue making progress on this journey, and you'll unleash the full potential of your 50+ cohort for more effective strategy execution, while at the same time gaining an unprecedented competitive advantage.

---

91 https://futureready.org/future-ready-frameworks/collaborative-leadership/
92 https://futureready.org/future-ready-frameworks/collaborative-leadership/
93 https://www.fairviewparkschools.org/departments/teaching-learning/future-ready-pledge
94 https://www.linkedin.com/pulse/what-future-ready-workforce-ashutosh-kumar

CHAPTER 10 SUMMARY

Designing a Wise Organization requires a dedicated focus on five areas and, if done right, will shape your competitive advantage and improve innovation, growth, and productivity. Start by creating awareness and excitement of what is possible, followed by diagnosing the status quo to build a baseline and create a roadmap for future success. As a second step, provide leaders in the organization with the appropriate insights and skills to enhance their leadership effectiveness in an aging workforce. The third area focuses on enabling your mature workers to identify a new sense of purpose and work contribution in the context of their respective role and the strategy of the firm. The fourth area looks at aligning talent management processes to better leverage the potential of the aging workforce. Finally, shape and embrace an inspired culture and mindset to seamlessly sync all initiatives and actions to achieve your corporate goals—enabled by the unleashed potential of the demographic shift in the organization.

Blueprint and Task List for Creating a Wise Organization

Inspired 'Wise' Culture and Mindset

LEADERS	PEOPLE	PROCESSES
Insight / Skill / Commitment	Purpose/Experience/ Value Contribution	Adjustment / Alignment

ORGANIZATION
Awareness - Clarity - Aspiration

© WiseForce Advisors

Organization:
– Create awareness and excitement for getting to know and understand older workers.
– Diagnose the status quo within the organization.
– Build a roadmap for the future.
Leaders:
– Share insight learned through diagnostics.
– Provide comprehensive leadership training.

People: Enable mature workers to identify a new sense of purpose and work contribution.

Processes: Align talent management efforts to leverage the potential of older workers.

Culture & Mindset: Sync all Wise Management initiatives to corporate goals.

Chapter 11
Bridge the Age Gap: Managing the Multigenerational Workforce

Taylor, the SVP of Operations for a Fortune 500 company, realized he had to refocus management's attention on the aging workforce. One Thursday in November, he met his HR colleague, Sabine, for lunch. Sabine had done a bit of her own research about managing a multi-generational workforce, and she understood that any initiative had to address three elements:

- Meet the needs of aging workers.
- Integrate them into the organization.
- Facilitate interactions among different generations in the workplace.

"My takeaway from reading up on this topic is that it's about leveraging age-related differences. Think about it: What if we actually turned these age differences into unique strengths? The company would benefit from a more capable workforce, while we enhance the wellbeing of our mature talent," she explained to Taylor. It dawned on Taylor that ignoring the multigenerational aspect of this demographic shift could create or widen an unnecessary divide between young and old, leading to (or cementing) age-based stereotypes.

As the lunch meeting went on, Taylor and Sabine discussed the benefits of an age-diverse workforce. They also worried that some of their colleagues were losing patience with the company's intense focus on its DEI stance.

Taylor continued: "Don't we have issues in engineering and quality? But all we do is to focus on complying with our diversity objectives, instead of solving the problem. We are ticking the box instead of leveraging the experience of our mature workforce and the latest technology that some of our younger colleagues are mastering."

"You are spot on, Taylor," Sabine responded. "What if we could mobilize the organization's power from within and look at our quality issues with a fresh pair of 'intergenerational eyes.'"

Immediately, Taylor started spinning ideas for how to apply the diverse perspectives of different levels of experience and socialization to their Total Quality Management (TQM). He envisioned using AI more effectively in the firm's TQM practices and improving data-driven and experience-based decision-making; reframing the sustainability aspect of TQM; challenging the current level of agile responses to changing customer demands seen from the different generational perspectives; and last, but not least, benefitting from empowering employees and utilizing cross-functional teams.

Taylor and Sabine both agreed that the well-intentioned goal of promoting age diversity could have unintended consequences: Instead of prioritizing the business problem, they were prioritizing a principle (diversity) and losing focus on solving the root problem. They were energized by the thought of re-prioritizing quality around a powerful solution: the potential of intergenerational synergies. Sabine and Taylor decided to skip the coffee after lunch and start working immediately on implementing these ideas.

In the following months, new patterns of problem-solving, risk management, improved customer service, accelerated learning, and innovation emerged. Sabine and Taylor were instrumental in bridging the age gap in their organization. They saw how a holistic approach to age management (which you now understand to be a Wise Management approach) could help develop a new understanding of workplace cohesiveness, leading to higher productivity, employee satisfaction, and wellbeing. Pursuing this multigenerational approach would help them develop a sustainable competitive edge for the company.

In this way, Wise Management not only helps organizations unleash newfound productivity by tapping into the experience of older workers, but it also bridges the age gaps among different generations to help them work better together:

The key characteristics of each age group can be summarized as follows:[95]

1. **Traditionalists** (currently 75+ years old): loyal, disciplined workers who value structure and clear hierarchies
2. **Baby Boomers** (currently 59–75 years old): goal-oriented employees who appreciate in-person interaction and are motivated by rewards and promotions
3. **Generation X** (currently 43–58 years old): independent, adaptable workers who value work-life balance and efficiency
4. **Millennials** (currently 27–42 years old): tech-savvy, achievement-oriented individuals focused on meaningful work and career development
5. **Generation Z** (currently 18–26 years old): digital natives who prioritize salary, innovation, and social interaction in the workplace

Each generation brings unique strengths and perspectives, contributing to a diverse and dynamic work environment.[96]

Generation Alpha (born after 2010) has not yet entered the labor market. Generation Alpha is growing up in a highly digitalized world, where social media plays a central role. Digital filters and image editing programs can lead to a distorted self-perception, especially among younger generations. The constant use of social media and the ability to present oneself have become the norm for Generation Alpha. There is a risk that comparing oneself to idealized self-presentations of others on social media can have negative effects on self-esteem. It may be crucial for future Generation Alpha workers to distinguish consciously between digital self-presentation and genuine self-perception. This will have a profound impact on their ability to fit into an intergenerational workforce, and likewise for their leaders to integrate and support them.

95   https://www.betterup.com/blog/generations-in-the-workplace and https://vervoe.com/age-diversity/
96   https://employsure.com.au/blog/benefits-of-age-diversity-in-the-workplace

As complex as the workplace has become, there are two key leadership behaviors helping to bridge the generational gap and to manage five generations in the workplace: The first is empathy.[97] The second is to help each individual to understand how to experience being part of the achieved success. The latter is particularly important for the 50+ workforce, as this group has experienced numerous times how it feels when you are not considered to be part of the future.

In addition to these two key leadership behaviors, there are a dozen or more drivers for a successful multigenerational workplace:[98]

1. **Inclusive communication:** Utilize diverse communication channels and styles to ensure all generations remain connected and informed.

2. **Flexible work arrangements:** Offer adaptable work options to accommodate various generational preferences and needs.

3. **Avoid stereotyping:** Treat each employee as an individual, rather than making assumptions based on generational stereotypes.

4. **Continuous learning and development:** Offer tailored training programs and encourage knowledge sharing across generations, through efforts such as reverse mentoring initiatives.

5. **Flexible work policies:** Implement adaptable work arrangements, including remote options and flexible scheduling, to cater to diverse generational needs.

6. **Cross-generational collaboration:** Form diverse teams that combine the experience of older employees with the innovative thinking of younger ones.

7. **Tailored motivation strategies:** Recognize and leverage the unique preferences and values of each generation to boost engagement.

8. **Technology integration:** Provide broad training on new technologies, and leverage the tech-savviness of younger generations.

97 https://www.google.de/books/edition/The_Empathy_Advantage/uHGxEAAAQBA-J?hl=en&gbpv=1&printsec=frontcover
98 https://www.disclo.com/resources/managing-a-multi-generational-workforce-a-comprehensive-guide-for-hr-professionals and https://meditopia.com/en/forwork/articles/tips-on-managing-multigenerational-workforce-in-world

9. **Mentorship programs:** Facilitate knowledge transfer and foster mutual understanding through cross-generational mentoring.

10. **Inclusive company culture:** Create an environment where all generations feel valued, respected, and empowered to contribute their unique talents.

11. **Diverse employee value proposition:** Offer a range of benefits and perks that appeal to different generational preferences.

12. **Emphasis on strengths:** Recognize and harness the unique strengths each generation brings to the workplace.

By focusing on these drivers, organizations can create a harmonious and productive multigenerational work environment that leverages the diverse talents and perspectives of all employees. Check out the perceived benefits that a multigenerational workforce brings according to a recent OECD survey:

Perceived benefits that a multigenerational workforce brings

Share of employers that have agreed or strongly agreed that multigenerational workforce brings a specific benefit

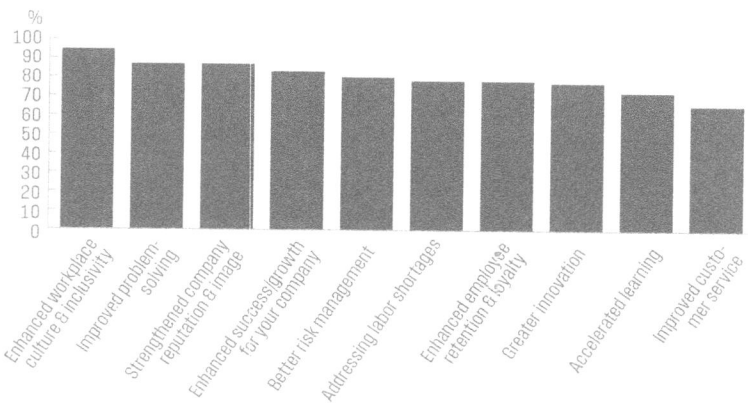

Note: 52 respondents among members of B4IG/WBCSD and BIAC.

Source: 2024 OECD/B4IG/WBCSD Multigenerational workforce survey. https://www.oecd.org/content/dam/oecd/en/topics/policy-issues/ageing-and-employment/Career-Paths-and-Engagement-

CHAPTER 11 SUMMARY

When organizations focus on unleashing the potential of an aging workforce, they may overlook the role of age gaps between "younger and older" employees. Wise Organizations are aware of the additional impact that effective management of age differences can have on company performance. Empathy and inclusiveness are key drivers for success.

Chapter 12
The Silver Standard: Measuring the Success of Wise Management

Greta and John, both VPs of Controlling for a sizable utility company, were chatting over coffee about how to measure the success of a Wise Organization, in which the potential of older workers in the organization was fully unleashed. Greta, a strong proponent of the firm's D&I initiatives, wondered whether success could be measured through this lens. John, on the other hand, considered the bigger picture of success across the company and wanted a way to measure results accordingly. As the meeting continued, both were contemplating whether success could only be measured for each initiative separately and later aggregated. For her part, Greta wasn't sure if one could measure certain indicators referring to the aging worker alone, in light of the interdependencies across all age groups.

After ordering another cup of coffee, John and Greta tried to reframe the question around the opportunity cost associated with poor or non-existing Wise Management. They selected the following six cost categories that could be used instead:

1. **Underutilized talent:** Failing to leverage the experience and knowledge of older employees can result in missed opportunities for innovation and mentorship.

2. **Skill obsolescence:** Older workers may face reduced productivity if their skills become outdated and they are not provided with training to update them.[99]

---

99   https://inzeko.ktu.lt/index.php/EE/article/download/7081/7168 and https://www.oecd-ilibrary.org/sites/59752153-en/1/3/5/index.html

3. **Knowledge loss:** When older employees retire without effective knowledge transfer, organizations can lose valuable institutional knowledge, impacting productivity.[100]
4. **Innovation decline:** Workforce aging can lead to lower levels of innovation and technology adoption, reducing overall productivity growth.[101]
5. **Health-related productivity loss:** Chronic health issues among older workers can lead to increased absenteeism and presenteeism, further reducing productivity.[102]
6. **Increased turnover:** Lack of support for older workers can lead to higher turnover rates, resulting in increased recruitment and training costs.

By the end of the conversation, Greta and John had landed on the idea of selecting indicators that more directly point to the engagement, value contribution, and leveraged potential of knowledge and expertise of a mature worker—and indeed, this is precisely what a Wise Organization is all about.

For John and Greta, the key was to use a combination of quantitative and qualitative measures to get a comprehensive view of the impact of their Wise Management strategies. Regular monitoring and analysis of these metrics can help companies refine their approaches and demonstrate the value of Wise Management initiatives. Here are the top 10 indicators that we suggest using:

Workforce Demographics Tracking

– Monitor the age profile of the company's workforce over time.
– Measure recruitment and hiring rates across different age groups.

100 https://inzeko.ktu.lt/index.php/EE/article/download/7081/7168
101 https://www.imf.org/external/pubs/ft/wp/2016/wp16238.pdf
102 https://bmcpublichealth.biomedcentral.com/articles/10.1186/s12889-022-14813-2 and https://www.ncbi.nlm.nih.gov/pmc/articles/PMC9976676/

- Monitor career progression and internal mobility rates across different age groups.

Skill Obsolescence Tracking

The most important cause of productivity loss due to poor age management is skill obsolescence. If you monitor and measure the impact of skill level on work output, you can prevent skills from becoming outdated and get ahead of the struggle as older workers try to adapt to new technologies and processes. This visibility will enable you to assess the need for upskilling or reskilling before it causes big problems. Skill obsolescence is compounded by challenges in knowledge transfer and adapting to changing job requirements.

Skills and Development Metrics

- Assess participation rates in training and development programs by age.
- Measure the skill acquisition and career progression of older workers.
- Track internal mobility and promotions across age groups.

Retention Metrics

- Monitor retention rates across different age groups to evaluate the effectiveness of Wise Management practices.
- Analyze cost savings from the reduced turnover of experienced workers.

Performance Metrics

- Compare productivity and performance metrics between age groups.
- Evaluate knowledge transfer and mentoring programs between generations.

Employee Satisfaction Surveys and Feedback

– Conduct regular employee satisfaction and engagement surveys across age groups.
– Use sentiment analysis from employee check-ins to gauge engagement levels.
– Gather feedback on age management initiatives through focus groups.

Health and Wellbeing Indicators

– Track absenteeism rates across age groups.
– Monitor usage of health and wellness programs by older workers.
– Measure work ability index scores for employees of different ages.

Organizational Culture Indicators

– Evaluate changes in age-related stereotypes and biases over time.
– Measure instances of age discrimination complaints.

External Recognition

– Monitor employer brand perception related to age diversity.

Succession Planning Effectiveness

– Evaluate the pipeline of talent across age groups for key roles.
– Assess knowledge retention from retiring workers.

By tracking these metrics, companies can gain insights into the effectiveness of their investment in Wise Management strategies and make data-driven decisions to improve their practices. Regularly reassess the organizational age climate and practices, and adjust strategies based on ongoing feedback and evaluation results.

CHAPTER 12 SUMMARY

Building a Wise Organization is a long process with many stakeholders involved, so the question of ROI is both instrumental for creating the right momentum and a measure for sustained success. Stakeholders who may be stuck between the dilemma of importance vs. urgency need to be confronted with "what if" questions and the implied burden of inaction. Stakeholders who are committed to shaping a Wise Organization need to look at the ROI of their actions—simply as a means of good business practice. But it is important to understand that there is not one single ROI number to focus on, but a combination of quantitative and qualitative measures that provides a comprehensive view of the impact of your Wise Management strategies and informs you about the effectiveness and potential adjustment needs.

Part Four:

The
Platinum Age

Chapter 13
Future-Proofing with Silver Foxes: Get Ahead of the Trend

When I met Jonathan, CEO of a market-leading Fortune 500 company—let's call it EnergCo—to discuss major business trends impacting the organization, we kicked off the conversation with some hard truths:

"Did you know that by 2100, populations in some major economies will fall by 20 percent to 50 percent, according to the UN?" I said. "And, while fertility is falling, people are living longer." I went on to explain that these trends were leading to inverted age structures — obelisks instead of pyramids — as the number of older people grows and the number of younger people shrinks. Whether they realize it or not, businesses already feel the tangible implications of an aging population.

"Jonathan," I continued, "by 2030, upwards of 150 million jobs will shift to workers over the age of 55, accounting for a quarter of the workforce."

Jonathan looked out the window, as he considered these statistics, wondering how and when they might start to affect EnergCo. Then he turned back to face me and said, "OK, you have my attention. Let's use the time today to talk about what we can do here to create awareness and a sense of urgency for dealing with this challenge. I want to know what steps you think we need to take now."

I pulled out recent studies from McKinsey, Bain & Co., and Roland Berger on the longevity imperative. All of the reports point to uncertainties around demographic change that will persist for decades. And they all suggest that societies and organizations need to prepare for this reality sooner rather than later.

From Jonathan's expression, I recognized a familiar question: "I wonder how EnergCo will be affected by these trends and how resilient we are as a firm?" he seemed to be thinking. Jonathan flipped through the papers, scanning for data and recommended actions. Then he put the reports down and said, "Let's get this done right. I want to start investigating our strategic options and which specific actions would yield the most promising impact in the short-, mid- and long-terms."

Conversations like this one are taking place now, all over the world, in every industry. As with any major change, there will be those who heed the warning and take steps now, and those who delay and pay the price later. Although the evidence is still limited, many pioneering companies have taken the first steps to meet the challenge of an aging workforce.

Albert Einstein famously said, "If I had an hour to solve a problem and my life depended on the solution, I would spend the first 55 minutes determining the proper question to ask... for once I know the proper question, I could solve the problem in less than five minutes."[1] In this section, I've outlined starter questions for each leadership role:

If you are the **chairperson** of a company, ask the CEO this question:

What strategic plans are in place to retain and leverage the skills and knowledge of our older employees while ensuring a smooth transition for future workforce needs?

This question addresses key concerns such as knowledge retention, succession planning, and adapting work environments to support older workers. It also prompts consideration of how to maintain productivity and competitiveness amid demographic changes.

If you are the **CEO** of an organization, your main question to the executive board should be:

What is our strategic plan for sustainability, succession management, and knowledge transfer to mitigate the impact of retiring Baby Boomers on leadership and workforce continuity?

---

1   https://amorebeautifulquestion.com/einstein-questioning/

This question addresses the need for proactive succession planning, retention of institutional knowledge, and preparation of younger talent to fill key roles, ensuring a smooth transition and sustained organizational performance.

If you are the **CHRO** of your company, ask yourself the following question when faced with an aging workforce:

How can we effectively retain, support, and transition older employees while ensuring engagement, knowledge transfer, and workforce sustainability?

Key focus areas include addressing health and wellness needs, bridging technology and skill gaps, implementing flexible work arrangements, fostering an inclusive culture, and creating robust succession planning strategies to mitigate potential loss of institutional knowledge and to maintain productivity.

And if you are the company's **CFO**, start the conversation with one of these four questions:

How can we balance cost management with employee retention? We must find ways to manage rising costs while retaining valuable experienced employees.

What are the implications for our compensation expenses? Older workers often command higher salaries due to their experience and tenure, which can affect labor costs and profitability.

How much should we invest in reskilling and upskilling programs for older workers?

What are the financial implications of potential gaps between employee retirement savings and actual needs?

By addressing these questions, senior stakeholders and leaders can develop strategies to mitigate economic risks and leverage the benefits of an experienced workforce in a dynamic business environment.

While the macro data is clear—the world is getting older and people are living longer—your organization may not yet consider itself to have an aging workforce. Here are some telltale signs that indicate a need for immediate action:

1. **Age demographics:** Workers aged 50 and older are the benchmark for defining an aging workforce due to their proximity to retirement and unique workplace needs.[2]

2. **Proportion of older workers:** When a significant percentage of the workforce is aged 50 or older (e.g., exceeding 30 percent of the total workforce), it may be time to think about strategic interventions.

3. **Increased absenteeism:** If you notice employees needing more time off for health-related issues, you may have an aging workforce.[3]

4. **Adaptability:** If you observe more employees having difficulty adapting to new technologies or processes, this can indicate that the senior segment of the workforce is growing.

5. **Knowledge retention risks:** If your organization has a high number of people reaching retirement, you may be at risk of losing valuable institutional knowledge.

6. **Recruitment and succession gaps:** As the workforce ages, new challenges can arise with recruiting younger talent to replace retiring employees or fill critical roles.[4]

7. **Economic pressures:** Rising costs associated with healthcare, pensions, or workplace accommodations for older employees also indicate a need for prompt attention.[5]

The most important resource in any economy or organization is its human capital—that is, the collective knowledge, attributes, skills, experience, and health of the workforce. But if the age distribution on an organizational level shifts toward more workers being older, and a population decline starts to set in (as we're now seeing in most indus-

---

2   https://www.oecd.org/en/data/indicators/employment-rate-by-age-group.html
3   https://www.cdc.gov/niosh/aging/data-research/index.html
4   https://www.leuphana.de/en/portals/later-life-workplace-index.html
5   https://www.work-fit.com/blog/aging-workforce-challenges-opportunities

trialized countries), the labor participation rate won't increase, and the organization will feel the impact of this shift at its core.[6]

By now, you can clearly see that the business case for building a Wise Organization is compelling (if not, go back to Chapter 3). But unlike other product- or market-related situations, in which there are established warning systems or relatable best practices that force organizations to action, it may be more difficult in this case to take the appropriate steps that will future-proof the organization.

Are we dealing with a "boiling frog" syndrome? The boiling frog syndrome in humans is a metaphor that describes the gradual habituation to negative or dangerous situations, often leading to detrimental outcomes. This concept is based on the anecdote of a frog that fails to jump out of slowly heating water, eventually leading to its demise.

The gradual shift of age demographics matters a lot. Inaction will lead to economic consequences as detailed earlier in this book: skills and labor shortages, loss in valuable experiences, reduced innovation, higher turnover cost, and decreased productivity.

Even so, many organizations are finding it difficult to get started, let alone build momentum. I wanted to understand how this challenge compares to other transformation initiatives around sustainability and diversity. I first looked at the example of climate change.

Sustainability Strategies

In Chapter 8, we introduced the idea that the aging phenomenon has similarities with climate change initiatives and sustainability transformations. Here are some further thoughts on this comparison:

Complexity and Scale

Both issues are complex, large-scale problems that affect entire societies. Climate change impacts global ecosystems and human sys-

---

6   https://www.mckinsey.com/capabilities/people-and-organizational-performance/our-insights/human-capital-at-work-the-value-of-experience#/

tems across the world.[7] Population aging is occurring in almost every country, with the proportion of people over 65 projected to rise from 9 percent to 16 percent globally by 2050.[8] These challenges require comprehensive, long-term strategies that are difficult to implement quickly.

Long-Term Planning

Tackling these issues requires long-term thinking and planning: The effects of climate change and population aging unfold over decades, making it challenging to maintain consistent policy focus and public attention.[9] Solutions for both often require immediate action for benefits that may not be fully realized immediately.

Public Awareness and Action

Both issues create challenges for mobilizing public awareness and action: The gradual nature of climate change can make it difficult for people to perceive immediate threats or the need for urgent action. The same applies to organizations that perceive the threats of a shifting age distribution as happening far in the future, if at all.

On an organizational level, I have found that understanding the "knowing-doing gap" can explain inaction and provide a framework to turn hesitancy into action.

The Knowing-Doing Gap

According to the International Society of Neuro Semantics, the knowing-doing gap describes the discrepancy between what we know and what we actually do.[10] This gap stems from several psychological factors:

---

7 https://academic.oup.com/heapro/article/39/2/daae031/7639701
8 https://ysph.yale.edu/news-article/aging-population-to-be-major-driver-of-future-climate-related-deaths/
9 https://www.helpage.org/news/climate-change-in-an-ageing-world/
10 https://www.neurosemantics.com/the-knowing-doing-gap/

1. **Fear:** People often avoid taking action due to fear of complexity, risk, mistakes, competition, and the unknown.[11] This fear can lead to paralysis and inaction, even when we possess the necessary knowledge.

2. **Complacency:** Individuals may become comfortable with their current situations, leading to a lack of motivation to implement changes or new knowledge.[12]

3. **Avoidance:** Some people tend to avoid challenging tasks or situations, preferring to remain in their comfort zones rather than applying new knowledge.[13]

4. **Wishful thinking:** The belief that merely possessing knowledge is sufficient for success can prevent individuals from taking concrete actions.[14]

5. **Procrastination:** Delaying action due to various reasons, such as perfectionism or lack of immediate urgency, contributes to the knowing-doing gap.[15]

6. **Cognitive dissonance:** The discomfort experienced when trying new behaviors that don't feel authentic can lead people to revert to familiar patterns.[16]

7. **Substituting talk for action:** Many individuals mistake discussing, planning, or measuring for actual action, creating a false sense of progress.[17]

8. **Automatic behavior:** Fatigue, burnout, and pressure to meet deadlines can cause people to default to old habits rather than implementing new knowledge.[18]

11 https://www.tobysinclair.com/post/book-summary-knowing-doing-gap
12 https://thesoulconnection.com.au/blog/8-knowing-doing-gap-reasons/
13 https://thesoulconnection.com.au/blog/8-knowing-doing-gap-reasons/
14 https://thesoulconnection.com.au/blog/8-knowing-doing-gap-reasons/
15 https://thesoulconnection.com.au/blog/8-knowing-doing-gap-reasons/
16 https://www.lizgooster.com/2016/09/09/bridging-the-knowing-doing-gap/
17 https://lifeisalaboratory.com/the-knowing-doing-gap/
18 https://www.tobysinclair.com/post/book-summary-knowing-doing-gap

9. **Fear of failure:** The anxiety associated with potential mistakes or imperfections can prevent individuals from taking risks and applying their knowledge.[19]
10. **Lack of clear implementation strategies:** Without specific, actionable steps, people may struggle to translate their knowledge into concrete behaviors.[20]

For an example of the "knowing-doing gap" at work, let's look at a situation that the global head of HR for a $2B revenue specialty chemical company employing over 4,000 people experienced. I'll refer to her as Beth. One day, Beth decided to use her weekly meeting to discuss challenges related to the firm's aging workforce with her boss, the company's CEO. Beth prepared a thorough presentation, covering the bigger picture, company data, and potential implications for the firm. The CEO's reaction was short: "I believe in recruiting young talent. There's no reason to keep the older employees."

With this kind of attitude, the CEO clearly is not considering the thinning talent market, as well as the growing percentage of his 50+ workforce that needs to be managed differently. And Beth? She came away discouraged and unlikely to bring this subject up again any time soon.

Understanding these psychological barriers is crucial for bridging the knowing-doing gap and translating knowledge into action, so your organization can become ready for the aging phenomenon. To future-proof their organization, some leaders might want to draw on their previous successes with challenges that were similarly complex and encompassed the entire organization. Here are some key takeaways from sustainability strategies:

---

19   https://www.neurosemantics.com/the-knowing-doing-gap/
20   https://www.tobysinclair.com/post/book-summary-knowing-doing-gap

Strategic Alignment and Integration

One of the most critical lessons from sustainability transformation initiatives is the importance of aligning sustainability goals with the organization's broader mission and values.[21] Successful organizations integrate sustainability into their corporate strategy and culture rather than treating it as a separate initiative. This holistic approach ensures that sustainability becomes a core part of the business rather than an afterthought.

Continuous Evaluation and Improvement

Organizations now understand that sustainability is an ongoing process that requires regular evaluation and adjustment. Accordingly, successful companies continuously measure performance against established sustainability goals, review and improve their strategies regularly, and implement effective countermeasures when results don't meet expectations.[22] This approach allows for agility and ensures the sustainability strategy remains relevant and effective.

Stakeholder Engagement

Engaging stakeholders throughout the sustainability journey is crucial. Many organizations have discovered that clear communication of how short-term objectives contribute to the long-term sustainability vision builds trust, how transparency in reporting progress and challenges is essential,[23] and how customizing communication for different stakeholder groups improves engagement and support.[24]

Resource Allocation and Leadership

Successful implementation requires proper resource allocation and strong leadership commitment. Organizations often find that dedicated teams and adequate budgets are necessary to drive initiatives forward—and also that leadership's commitment is crucial in steering sustainability efforts across all levels of the organization.[25]

Employee Involvement and Training

Organizations know that involving employees at all levels is vital for success. This includes providing education and training on sustainability issues, encouraging active participation and commitment to sustainability efforts,[26] and linking incentives and rewards to sustainable outcomes to foster alignment.[27]

Innovation and Opportunities

Implementing sustainability strategies often leads to unexpected benefits. For example, organizations report discovering new opportunities for innovation in products and processes, potential for cost reductions and revenue growth, and access to new markets and investment capital.[28]

Data-Driven Approach

Successful organizations learn to ground their sustainability goals in scientific rigor; to use clear, quantifiable, and time-bound targets; and to leverage data to track progress and inform decision-making.[29]

25 https://dazzle-platform.com/blog/the-4-sails-of-successful-sustainability-strategy-implementation/

26 https://www.rostoneopex.com/resources/sustaining-success-a-roadmap-through-the-5-essential-stages-of-a-sustainability-action-plan

27 https://kaizen.com/insights/importance-corporate-sustainability-strategy/

28 https://www.prosci.com/blog/change-management-for-sustainability

29 https://plana.earth/academy/communicating-sustainability-strategy-transparency-responsibility

Post-Implementation Review

Organizations often find value in conducting thorough post-implementation reviews. These reviews help to identify lessons learned and best practices, create knowledge repositories for future projects, and enhance overall project management capabilities.[30]

Sustainability strategies indicate a company's commitment to long-term viability and proactive responses to industry changes.[31] This forward-thinking approach can improve a company's resilience and adaptability in a rapidly changing business environment. The same applies to embracing the concept of a Wise Organization.

One key difference between sustainability transformation and aging-ready initiatives is that the Corporate Sustainability Reporting Directive (CSRD) requires companies to disclose this nonfinancial information as part of their reporting on environmental, social, and governance (ESG) matters.[32] The directive enhances transparency and accountability regarding sustainability practices, empowering stakeholders with comprehensive insights into a company's ESG performance. By comparison, age management does not have the backing of government regulation at this time.

DEI Strategies

The DEI movement has faced several challenges that have limited its impact in organizations. By examining these mistakes,[33] we can learn valuable lessons for shaping a Wise Organization:

---

30 https://www.pmworld360.com/effective-post-implementation-review-uncovering-5-secrets-to-success/

31 https://www.forbes.com/councils/forbesbusinesscouncil/2024/06/07/18-reasons-why-sustainability-can-be-a-strategic-business-advantage/

32 https://www.accenture.com/il-en/insights/consulting/esg-reporting-compliance-competitive-advantage

33 https://www.goco.io/blog/10-mistakes-hr-pros-make-with-dei-initiatives

Lack of Meaningful Action

One of the most significant issues is the implementation of empty DEI initiatives without real action or impact. Many organizations have adopted DEI efforts merely to "check the box" without genuine commitment to change. This approach leads to problems such as issuing statements and guidelines without follow-through, failing to coordinate with other departments for implementation, and neglecting to provide adequate training or clear expectations.

To address this scenario, organizations must ensure that leaders of DEI initiatives are passionate advocates and true allies who can drive meaningful change.

Insufficient Resource Allocation

DEI efforts often fail due to improper allocation of company resources, particularly time and money. To fix this, organizations need to prioritize DEI in budgeting and resource allocation, invest properly in people and community initiatives, and understand that DEI requires ongoing commitment, not just short-term projects.

One-Size-Fits-All Approach

Many organizations fail to employ a standardized approach to DEI, failing to recognize the distinct needs of different marginalized communities. To improve, they found that it helps to tailor DEI strategies to address the specific challenges of various groups and to avoid generalizing experiences across all underrepresented communities.

Lack of Structural Change

DEI initiatives often focus on individual awareness without addressing the root causes of inequity. To create lasting impact, we've learned that leaders must address structural inequalities that sustain discriminatory culture, implement clear processes for dealing with workplace discrimination, and focus on changing organizational systems—not just individual mindsets.

Insufficient Institutional Power

DEI practitioners often lack the authority to implement the necessary changes.[34] To empower DEI efforts, companies need to grant DEI leaders decision-making power equivalent to other executives, ensure DEI teams have resources to make organization-wide changes, and avoid relegating DEI solely to junior-level employees or committees.

Lack of Accountability

Many organizations set DEI goals without genuine intention to achieve them.[35] To address this problem, leaders must hold those in positions of power accountable for DEI outcomes, and implement systems to track and measure progress on DEI objectives.

Surface-Level Initiatives

Organizations often resort to superficial DEI activities that fail to address systemic issues.[36] Those that succeed do so by moving beyond cultural celebrations and unconscious bias training, focusing on interventions that resolve root causes of inequities, and being willing to overhaul the policies and practices that cause harm.

Difficulty in Measuring Impact

The challenge of quantifying DEI's impact on organizational performance can limit investment.[37] To address this, leading companies develop clear and consistent metrics to demonstrate DEI's value. They also create indicators that can show the effectiveness of DEI efforts.

---

34 https://www.linkedin.com/pulse/5-ways-dei-has-been-ineffective-how-we-make-better-asare-ph-d--eaime

35 https://www.linkedin.com/pulse/5-ways-dei-has-been-ineffective-how-we-make-better-asare-ph-d--eaime

36 https://www.linkedin.com/pulse/5-ways-dei-has-been-ineffective-how-we-make-better-asare-ph-d--eaime

37 https://www.forbes.com/sites/carolinamilanesi/2023/04/20/the-business-impact-of-diversity-equity-and-inclusion/

Lack of Sustained Commitment

DEI efforts often fail due to a lack of long-term commitment from leadership.[38] To ensure success, they have to secure ongoing support from top management; treat DEI as an ongoing process, not a one-time initiative; and continuously improve and adapt DEI strategies over time

By learning from these DEI challenges and mistakes, organizations can develop more effective, impactful, and sustainable initiatives to future-proof the company for the era of aging.

A final word on the critical role of the board

As the demographic shift reaches center stage, a new level of responsibility is emerging for corporate boards. Since traditional board composition does not clearly assign responsibility for this issue to a specific role, it becomes the chairperson's role to assume the initial responsibility for this topic. The chair of the board should take the following steps:

1. Increase awareness and urgency.
2. Educate board members on this subject with a focus on its strategic relevance.
3. Help to break through competing priorities.
4. Address cultural biases and discrimination implications.

To assure that this systemic and global change affecting all organizations is addressed systematically, existing board governance codes could include the aging workforce as part of good governance. Here are some examples of codes that align with the topic of aging:

G20/OECD Principles of Corporate Governance

These principles aim to improve the legal, regulatory, and institutional framework for corporate governance, particularly for listed companies.

---

38 https://www.forbes.com/councils/theyec/2023/04/03/10-reasons-why-dei-efforts-fail-and-how-to-ensure-they-succeed/

They cover shareholder rights, corporate disclosure, board responsibilities, and sustainability.[39]

Goldman Sachs Corporate Governance Guidelines

Goldman Sachs has a set of principles designed to promote effective board functioning and shareholder interests, covering aspects like board composition and performance evaluation.[40]

UK Corporate Governance Code

This framework sets standards for corporate governance in the UK, focusing on leadership, effectiveness, accountability, remuneration, and shareholder relations. The code applies to companies listed on the London Stock Exchange and requires them to disclose their adherence or provide explanations for noncompliance.[41]

Together, the board and the entire senior leadership of any organization are responsible for tackling the challenge of this impending demographic shift. The call to action is simple: Apply a Wise mindset to the problem and turn your seasoned employees into an unbeatable competitive advantage. Getting Wise is all about unleashing power from within. It's a must-do because if you don't take action, your competitors most certainly will.

39 https://www.oecd.org/en/topics/corporate-governance.html
40 https://www.goldmansachs.com/investor-relations/corporate-governance/corporate-governance-documents/corp-gov-guidelines.pdf
41 https://www.frc.org.uk/library/standards-codes-policy/corporate-governance/uk-corporate-governance-code/

CHAPTER 13 SUMMARY

As you work toward future-proofing your organization to turn an aging workplace into a competitive advantage, each senior stakeholder must play a vital role. This process is about asking key questions that reveal how demographic change is affecting the organization in general, and in each specific area of responsibility. Ask yourself, "What can I do to develop strategies to mitigate economic risks while leveraging the benefits of an experienced workforce in a rapidly changing business environment?" Resolve to overcome the psychological barriers that prevent leaders from taking action, and get your organization ready for the future today. Leaders can further accelerate the process of future-proofing the organization by drawing on their successes with previous transformation challenges. Sustainability strategies are one area to explore in this way.

Chapter 14
The Wise Revolution: Pioneering the Future of Work

In 2024, Roland Berger, a global management consulting firm, published an article titled "Why leaders need a longevity strategy."[42]

A term called the "longevity economy" refers to the sum of all economic activities driven by people aged 50 and older, including their direct spending on goods and services as well as the additional economic activity this spending generates.[43] This concept encompasses the economic contributions and potential of an aging population living longer, healthier lives.[44]

Longevity is transforming traditional demographic structures. By 2050, the number of people aged 60+ is expected to double to 2.1 billion.[45] Key aspects of the longevity economy include:

1. **Economic impact:** In 2020, the 50+ population contributed $45 trillion to global GDP, representing 34 percent of the total.[46]

2. **Spending power:** In the US, the spending power of those aged 50 and over reached $7.6 trillion in 2015.[47]

3. **Growth potential:** World Data Lab projects the spending growth of this group to be around 5.5 percent over the next decade.[48]

---

42 https://www.rolandberger.com/en/Insights/Publications/Why-leaders-need-a-longevity-strategy.html
43 https://www.aarpinternational.org/the-journal/current-edition/journal-articles-blog/2019/01/longevity-economy
44 https://www.aarpinternational.org/resources/longevity-economy/longevity-economy
45 https://www.rolandberger.com/en/Insights/Publications/Why-leaders-need-a-longevity-strategy.html
46 https://www.brookings.edu/articles/the-age-of-the-longevity-economy/
47 https://www.aarpinternational.org/the-journal/current-edition/journal-articles-blog/2019/01/longevity-economy
48 https://www.brookings.edu/articles/the-age-of-the-longevity-economy/

4. **Shift in economic sectors:** The longevity economy will see expansion in health and education sectors, along with the emergence of new financial products.[49]
5. **Employment and productivity:** Longevity aims to raise employment over the life course, boosting human capital and productivity as older workers maintain their skills for longer.[50]

The longevity economy challenges traditional views of aging populations as economic burdens, instead recognizing their substantial and increasing contributions to economic activity through labor, consumption, taxes, and nonmarket activities like volunteering and caregiving.[51]

Looking ahead, we can expect to see older people become increasingly important for workforces. In 1990, people between 45 and 64 accounted for 28 percent of the working-age population in OECD countries. That's now 40 percent.

For consumer businesses, there's an often-overlooked opportunity in an aging population—spending power. According to AARP, a US-based nonprofit focused on aging, the 50+ generation already accounts for half of global consumer spending. By 2050, this will reach nearly 60 percent, or $96 trillion. Despite these impressive numbers, many organizations still under-appreciate the importance of older generations, both as workers and consumers.

When we underestimate the capacity of older people, we exclude them from economic and social activity, and we underinvest in our own later years. That is a major problem as we live longer lives.

When speaking of "the future of work," we typically refer to a projection of how work, workers, and the workplace will evolve in the years ahead. Given unfolding evidence of the longevity economy, the "future of work" will be shaped by aging.

---

49 https://www.thelancet.com/journals/lanhl/article/PIIS2666-7568(21)00250-6/fulltext
50 https://www.thelancet.com/journals/lanhl/article/PIIS2666-7568(21)00250-6/fulltext
51 https://www.aarpinternational.org/resources/longevity-economy/longevity-economy

Smart leaders recognize that they need to prepare their organizations for the longevity economy, as the potential dividends are huge and missing out means risking the future of the business. And it goes without saying that becoming a Wise Organization is an excellent first step to navigating the opportunities along the longevity journey.

When you make a conscious choice to participate in the longevity economy, your organization becomes affiliated with social change, leading to further psychological benefits and motivations for evolving the Wise Organization early:

Psychological Reasons for Early Participation

Enhanced Collective Identity

Organizations that join social movements early often experience a strengthened sense of collective identity. This shared identity fosters a deeper connection among members and aligns the organization with a larger cause.[52]

Increased Collective Efficacy

Early participation can boost an organization's belief in its ability to effect change. This sense of collective efficacy motivates continued involvement and can lead to more ambitious goals.[53]

Moral Conviction and Values Alignment

Organizations may be driven by a strong moral conviction or a desire to align their actions with their core values. Joining a movement early demonstrates a commitment to these principles.[54]

---

52   https://www.frontiersin.org/journals/psychology/articles/10.3389/fpsyg.2023.1096877/full

53   https://www.frontiersin.org/journals/psychology/articles/10.3389/fpsyg.2023.1096877/full

54   https://pmc.ncbi.nlm.nih.gov/articles/PMC10162496/

Emotional Engagement

Social movements often evoke strong emotions, which can be a powerful motivator for organizational involvement. Early participation allows organizations to tap into this emotional energy.[55]

Benefits of Early Participation

Credibility and Legitimacy

Organizations that join movements early are likely to gain increased credibility and legitimacy in the eyes of the public and other stakeholders.[56]

Positive Psychological Changes

Successful participation in social movements can lead to positive changes in emotions, social identity, and values for both the organization and its members.[57]

Empowerment and Influence

Early involvement can empower organizations, giving them a greater sense of agency and potentially more influence in shaping the movement's direction.[58]

Network Expansion

Joining a movement early provides opportunities to build relationships with other like-minded organizations and individuals, expanding the organization's network and potential for collaboration.[59]

---

55 https://citizenshandbook.org/movements.html
56 https://sdgwatcheurope.org/how-can-ngos-connect-and-engage-more-with-social-movements/
57 https://www.frontiersin.org/journals/psychology/articles/10.3389/fpsyg.2023.1096877/full
58 https://www.frontiersin.org/journals/psychology/articles/10.3389/fpsyg.2023.1155950/full
59 https://www.sbcguidance.org/understand/social-movements

Innovation and Adaptability

Early participation can foster innovation within the organization as it adapts to new challenges and strategies associated with the movement.[60]

At this point, I hope I've convinced you that building a Wise Organization will unlock the power of age in your business and enable your organization to thrive in the longevity economy.

CHAPTER 14 SUMMARY

The longevity economy will shape the future of work. Smart organizations and their leaders will benefit from accepting this reality and embracing the concept of a Wise Organization, as depicted in this book. The returns on this investment will be significant. Choosing to become part of the longevity economy, by unlocking the potential of your aging workforce, is a prerequisite to getting ahead of the curve, building momentum for a new competitive advantage, and leapfrogging the competition.

---

60   https://www.frontiersin.org/journals/psychology/articles/10.3389/fpsyg.2023.1155950/full

Thank you!

As you close this book, I want to express my deepest gratitude for reading along and embarking on this journey to explore the intricate web of demographic shifts and their profound implications for organizations. Your commitment to understanding and addressing this complex issue is crucial for shaping our collective future—as well as the future of your organization and your personal experience in the world economy.

It has been an honor to share my thoughts, experiences, and insights with you. I hope that the pages you've turned have inspired, challenged, and perhaps even transformed you in some way.

If you have questions, reflections, or simply want to share your thoughts about this book, I would love to hear from you. You can reach me through my website at [Wiseforceadvisors.com], or connect with me on social media at [https://www.linkedin.com/in/christian-jerusalem]. I am always eager to engage with readers and explore new ideas together. Thank you!

Bibliographical Information of the German National Library
The German National Library lists this publication in the German National Bibliography. Detailed bibliographical data can be accessed on the internet at http://dnb.dnb.de.

Paperback: ISBN 978-1-968619-29-9
Hardcover: ISBN 978-1-968619-30-5
Ebook: ISBN 978-1-968619-31-2

Christian Jerusalem
Wise Up!
1ˢᵗ Edition 2025

© 2025 Lexware GmbH & Co. KG
Munzinger Str. 9, 79111 Freiburg

Cover design: Florin Preußler, Munich
Image credits (cover flap): WiseForce Advisors

Text editing and proofreading: Leinhäuser Language Services GmbH
Product Management: Elisabeth Heueisen

www.ingramcontent.com/pod-product-compliance
Lightning Source LLC
Chambersburg PA
CBHW040754220326
41597CB00029BA/4771